Thinking It Through:
A Practical Guide
to Academic
Essay Writing

Thinking It Through: A Practical Guide to Academic Essay Writing

Second Edition

Heather Avery
Lucille Strath
Karen Taylor
Kathleen James-Cavan

Catherine Taylor
Annette Tromly
Stephen Brown

Academic Skills Centre
Trent University
Peterborough, 1989

Thinking It Through: A Practical Guide to Academic Essay Writing

Academic Skills Centre
Trent University, Peterborough, Ontario. K9J 7B8

Printed in Canada by Webcom.
Printing of the First Edition 1987

Copyright © 1989
Includes appendices, answer keys and instructor's guide, and index

Permissions Granted

Humanities Index. April 1987–March 1988, Volume 14, page 854. Copyright © 1988 by the H.W. Wilson Company. Material reproduced on page 42 of this text by permission of the publisher.

Biological Abstracts. January 1989, Volume 87. Material reproduced on page 43 of this text by permission. Copyright BIOSIS. Reproduced with permission.

Historical Abstracts. DIALOG, file 39. Material on pages 50 and 51 of this text reproduced by permission. Copyright ABC-CLIO.

Canadian Cataloguing in Publication Data

Thinking it through

2nd ed.
ISBN 0-9693668-3-3

1. Essay.   2. Exposition (Rhetoric).   3. English language - Rhetoric.
I. Avery, Heather.   II. Trent University. Academic Skills Centre.

PE1471.T55 1989   808'.042   C89-094813-5

Table of Contents

Preface to the Second Edition

The first edition of *Thinking It Through* has enjoyed wide acceptance. Since its publication in the summer of 1987, many senior secondary and university students have found it a useful guide to purposeful, critical, and creative essay writing. At the time of its writing, the authors of the text shared several principles of composition theory and practice. They were:

> that students will learn the particulars of writing if they understand the principles; they will discover "how," if they are told "why";

> that the essay-writing process can be both linear and recursive, and that the combination of these progressive and evolutionary methods accurately reflects what takes place in making and communicating meaning;

> that while a thesis is something "set down," it is not static; it is an idea full of life and vigour which binds the essay together, propels it forward, and discloses itself.

Our workshop teaching, one-to-one counselling, and discussions with colleagues have led us to re-affirm these principles and to renew our efforts to find additional ways to put them into practice. We found that there were certain points in the writing process that students found particularly difficult. Some students were writing insubstantial papers because they were unfamiliar with research techniques; others, who were excellent organizers, could not record their thoughts; still others were handing in unpolished essays because they had not revised their drafts for a prospective reader. Moreover, the essay assignment is defined by an important, inescapable fact: behind every essay, there is a reader, and beyond that, a grade. Therefore, in response to these writing problems, the current authors of *Thinking It Through* have revised the first edition in several important ways.

This edition places greater emphasis on research. What we have attempted to provide is a clear, concise introduction to academic information gathering, notetaking, and documentation. The chapters on research and notetaking take much of the mystery out of what has often been a student's greatest barrier to independent study.

The former chapter on organization has been revised. The new chapter on prewriting and the one on drafting attempt to guide the student to the discovery that we write to find out what we want to say, that critical analysis does not precede writing but is an integral part of it: thinking and writing take place concurrently. These chapters also help the student to see that outlines and structure are not imposed on thought but are, like writing, acts of the imagination. In addition, the methods we suggest are based on the belief that, at the prewriting and drafting stages, it is necessary for students to withhold their critical sense of conventional grammar and syntax in order to allow their creative sense enough freedom to compose a way into a topic.

The chapter on revision is an important reorganization of the former text. It reflects the importance of the post-draft process in preparing the essay for its chosen audience, and suggests ways to re-see the essay and render it into comprehensible, persuasive order and language.

An index has been added to help the student and the instructor locate sections and key points. Checklists have been highlighted for easy identification. Another very attractive feature of the new book is its binding: it is bound in such a way that the book can lie flat, making it much easier to use for both the instructor leading a workshop and the student working independently.

The authors would like to say to instructors who are currently using *Thinking It Through* in their classrooms that we hope you will find these revisions helpful. We value the comments that many of you offered and, in some cases, your suggestions have been instrumental in bringing about the changes and additions that we have made.

And to students using this guide for the first time, we acknowledge that the idea of searching for essay topics during the first week of classes may not be appealing, yet we urge you to do so. We hope you will see essay writing as an important step toward personal independence, taking control and being responsible for what you know, and toward recognizing how useful and creative your new knowledge can be for you and for the intellectual community of which you are now a part. Imagine the essayist — you — with selected books, a framework of ideas taking shape, on the verge of a new discovery. Make no mistake. Essay writing is not easy, and it is not easy because every essay is new, a foray into the unknown. An essay is your organized, carefully conceived and sustained thought on a subject, brought together for the first time in exactly this way. The marked essay, then, reflects more than a grade; it charts the progress you have made toward greater and fuller independence. You do not know what you are capable of. As you write you will discover yourself, and surely this is the most demanding and the most rewarding of all human pursuits.

Despite the revisions we have made, this new version of *Thinking It Through* does not depart greatly, either in philosophy or content, from the first edition. The work and thought of the original writers still dominates the text, and we gratefully acknowledge their contributions.

This book began ten years ago as a manual for a short course on essay writing. Peter Slade, who was the Coordinator of the Academic Skills Centre when the course began, wrote a considerable amount of the original exercise material and deserves recognition, as do Richard Harrison, Isobel Henniger, Kari Lie, and Sheree-Lee Powsey, all of whom assisted with initial planning and writing.

In the summer of 1987, the manual material was revised and expanded into the first edition of *Thinking It Through*. Three individuals who have since left the Centre were responsible for much of this work. Catherine Taylor, the Project Head, used her quick wit and vivid writing style to shape many prosaic ideas about composition into a form that made them clear and meaningful to student readers. As well, her firm grasp of the creative possibilities in writing still informs the entire text. Annette Tromly, who was Coordinator of the Centre at that time, envisioned the project and worked long hours to see it through to completion. Finally, Stephen Brown's fascination with language and its rhythms contributed greatly to explanations in the text about how meaning is made. Our sincere appreciation goes to these three writers whose work provides the backbone of this revised text.

Thanks also must be extended to those individuals involved in the production of the second edition. Carol Tomlin, who helped to format and proofread the text, can take credit for consistency. Louis Taylor, Peter Northrop, Barbara Fox, and Barbara Pitt eased us through the transition from penned scribblings to typeset copy. Our gratitude to them, and to our many colleagues, both within Trent and outside that community, whose kind comments and thoughtful criticism helped to shape this revision. In particular, we appreciate the patient reading and thorough response of Deborah Berrill; her comments helped in the final polishing of the text.

It is our students, finally, who write texts such as this. Their queries and concerns shape our understanding of the writing process. Their responses determine what is included, what is excluded, what is emphasized. Thank you, then, to all those students who have participated viii

in our workshops and individual tutorials: we have relied heavily on your work. And finally, a special thanks to the three students who generously donated their essays to Appendix D of our text. We know that other students will benefit from seeing the results of their "thinking it through."

Thinking It Through

CHAPTER ONE

The Essay: Thinking It Through

Does life offer the student any prospect more daunting than the nasty gloom of deadlines? Surely the long essay is the most bullying of all professorial designs, deliberately contrived, so it seems, first to exasperate and finally to humiliate the student. Essay writing is very much an ordeal, unnatural in certain senses and always painful in the execution because it is a challenge to single combat, an exercise that demands self-commitment and fails without self-control. To begin to write is difficult, to persist exhausting; to conclude requires a spry wit and a fresh mind when you are least likely to possess either.

All kinds of work take their toll on the worker. But the peculiar stress that afflicts the writer comes not only from the outside forces of the assignment itself — the fear of not meeting the deadline, of falling in the professor's esteem, of failing the essay and then the course and as a result losing the B average required to get into law school — but also from the inward motions of self-discovery. The essay is inescapably a record of the life of its author, a map of the progress of one mind contemplating some part of the world it inhabits.

While the outside forces of deadlines do produce anxiety, the inward motions of self-discovery bring a deep sense of satisfaction. That pain and joy are inextricably entwined is one of life's paradoxes. The all-consuming nature of essay writing is the very thing that allows you to see beyond the ordinary and to measure the personal gains made by finally fixing on a page the new dimensions of what you think and know. Yes, it is hard work, but it is hard pleasurable work. The sense of accomplishment that comes from taking on the challenge of close research and communicating its results far exceeds all the difficulties you may have had.

History of the Essay

It is from the tradition of an individual thinking something through that the academic essay springs. The rise of the essay in European culture in the late sixteenth century was coincidental with the evolution of the notion of individual freedom and the increased recognition of the value of the self. For Montaigne and Frances Bacon, both as humanists and scientists (for neither man would have distinguished between the humanities and the sciences as we do), the essay was an explorative kind of writing – a laboratory of words, if you like. Montaigne named the new species from the French *essayer* ("to attempt") and he first assayed topics ranging from politics to theology, from cannibals to reflections on solitude, death, and marriage. Bacon's essays are less preoccupied with the inward explorations of his own mind than are those of Montaigne, and are given more to the examination of the outer world of nature in all its measurable and observable variety; he was, not surprisingly, the developer of the scientific method.

For both men the essay was the private voice of public experience, a personal and original mode of argumentation. Not only was the form of the essay new, but the use of prose was itself a fledgling endeavour in English. Prose writing encouraged a particularly personal spoken rhythm which lacked the formal restraints of metre and rhyme through which poems were written. It was more natural and less preconceived than poetry. The essay thus began as the simplest and most naturally reflective, self-generating, and self-sustaining kind of prose.

With the development of the periodical or journal essay and the rise of eighteenth-century prose stylists like Addison, Johnson, and Goldsmith, the essay became more widely public in its audience. The need for an objective voice and the difficulty of sustaining distance from one's own text became more prominent concerns of the essayist. The tone of the nineteenth-century essayist is discreetly public, and we seldom encounter an eccentrically private voice like that of Swift's Bickerstaff.

Still, the finest modern essayists (such as George Orwell, or closer to home, Elizabeth Hardwick), while managing to sustain a respectfully objective distance from the topic, have recognizable voices. Their private voices are addressed to a public audience in a way that does not permit the wandering off into the merely personal terrain of feelings, tastes, prejudices, and other autobiographical details. Yet, though the word "I" might not appear in it, the modern essay is personal: while the author may address the many, he or she remains only one individual talking. Whether that of the scientist or of the humanist, the language of the essayist is always and intimately expressive, a distinctly personal use of language generated by the unique unfolding of the idea pursued, more or less successfully, in each single exercise of writing. Essay writing is the art of channelling a private inner conversation between the mind and its subject into a public outer form, so that all essayists can say with Montaigne, "I am the text of my own book."[1]

The Academic Essay

Essays have become the primary means by which the community of scholars communicates. University professors, scientific researchers, practising lawyers and physicians, all publish essays in the journals of their own disciplines. Through the essay as journal article, scholars share their research findings, the results of their investigations, new ways of thinking about a subject that accommodate new evidence, and so on. In this way, working on essays at their own desks, they help to fulfill one of the primary functions of the university: to advance the growth of knowledge and understanding throughout the world community of scholars.

Clearly then, it is important that career academics learn to write essays well. But what is the point of imposing the burden on the vast majority of students who will become neither professors nor other publishing professionals? The answer lies in another of the overall aims of the academy: to teach students to think. The exercise of writing an essay provides the student with the best and most prolonged opportunity to think deeply and precisely into a subject; it also provides the professor with evidence of the student's ability to think. Essays are so important that students working for a B.A. may have to write as many as forty-five before receiving their degrees.

So what is a good university essay?

Many university students mistakenly think that the aim of university is to learn *things,* to acquire knowledge, to assimilate lots of information. That goal, taken to the extreme, would be dreary and self-defeating. Universities have been in operation for about eight hundred years now, and with the information explosion of our own electronic age, even the most modest university library holds more information than you could read if you outlived Methuselah. The goal, then, is not to devour the

---

[1]Michel de Montaigne, *Essays and Selected Writings,* ed. Donald M. Frame (New York: St. Martin's, 1963) 2.

library's holdings in your particular discipline, but to develop your analytical ability so that no matter what topic you have in mind, you will be able to think your way into it and bring back something valuable.

You will be evaluated not on what you know, but on how well you can think about what you know and on how well your writing elucidates that thought. Your instructors will be looking first for what ideas you can generate, what discriminations you can make, what interpretations you can develop, what arguments you can defend, what conclusions you can draw. These are signs of your ability to think in original and creative ways about the information you encounter. Do not instead set out to tell your reader everything in the world about the parts of the bullfrog or to enumerate every last instance of animal imagery in *Macbeth*. "This and this and this" tend to go in one ear and out the other because there is nothing to hold them all together. Such an attempt ends up in a sort of Five-&-Dime-catalogue approach: there is an impressive array of merchandise, but the only evidence of order is that all the hats are in one place and the toasters in another. "So what?" one might say, and the marker frequently does, in writing, beside a letter not among the first in the alphabet.

What an essay needs and a department store catalogue does not is a governing idea, some overall insight into the information presented that enables the reader to see how it all fits together. It is in discovering and developing a governing idea that you enter the essay, and the instructor will be looking for your presence just as he or she might look for evidence of thorough research. As a writer, then, you must take control. You choose what to emphasize; you look for patterns and relationships emerging and show how your insight or governing idea casts light on the topic. In some research-based essays, the information will be so prominent that your presence will be difficult to detect; in other papers, the argument is paramount, and your voice, persuading the reader of the soundness of your thesis, will echo throughout. Both kinds of essay, nonetheless, require that the writer remain firmly in control.

While an essay must bear the stamp of its author, its function is to contribute to a scholarly community, to encourage thought and re-examination. The essay thus must reflect self *and* acknowledge audience. A voice in the wilderness cannot be heard unless it is speaking comprehensibly, so at every stage the writer must struggle, not only to make meaning, but to make meaning clear.

It is more often lack of confidence than lack of effort that causes essays to go astray. People worry about their own capacities, believing all instructors to have brains more highly evolved than their own. They suppress their own interpretations, spend too much time doing research and not enough time thinking. They settle for the display of acquired knowledge rather than risk the attempt of doing something with it. Ultimately, this safe route is a dead end because it does not lead where you need to go. You must risk the New Jersey turnpike – full of cloverleafs and detours and homicidal New Yorkers though it may be. The academic essay is no place to be faint-hearted.

How, then, to ward off the anxiety and self-doubt that make students prefer the cul-de-sac to the bolder path? First, remind yourself that you are in school to learn, that your instructors do not expect undergraduate papers to rival their own scholarly achievements, that if they did you would be handed a diploma on the first day of your studies, not your last. Remember that writing is often messy, usually difficult, and more difficult some days than others. Take comfort in the assurance that you will get better and more efficient with practice. Work hard, but be as patient with yourself as if you were learning to play the violin.

Second, become methodical in your approach to the task of essay writing. Much of this book is devoted to planning and revising the essay. If you take the time to prepare properly and make the time to rewrite carefully, your essay will be better and the actual writing of the final draft both faster and less painful. The alternative is to try to perform simultaneously the conflicting feats of forecasting the overall development of the thesis and getting the right emphasis and wording for particular sentences. This task is akin to carving out the shortest route to the heart of the jungle without a map. In that attempt lies much of the dense overgrowth of anxiety, nausea, and crumpled paper familiar to those students who skimp on the planning stage of the essay.

The Essay-Writing Process

Over the course of our text we present the various aspects of the essay-writing process. The text commences by tackling the task of working from topic through to thesis. Chapters Three, Four, and Five explore in detail the complexities involved in compiling research and responding to the material accumulated. Chapters Six, Seven, and Eight deal with writing itself: preparing to write, drafting, and revising what has been written. In an appendix, we include the results of this process: three sample essays, one from the humanities, one from the sciences, one from the social sciences. These essays, although good, are not intended to be perfect. They are real undergraduate essays and represent the attempts of their authors to fulfill the demands of the essay. Students can learn from them, not only by using them as models, but also by evaluating them critically.

The process of writing an essay is both telescopic and recursive. It is telescopic in that it begins with a large and rather blurry view of a subject and moves purposefully toward successively more refined and detailed views. Refocusing is required at each shift to a new level of detail. The process is recursive in that it does not occur as a neat sequence of steps. The essayist should be looking for the thesis and trying to forecast the paper from very early in the planning stage, and refining, resketching, and revising often throughout the writing process. Remember that in an essay you are thinking an idea through; the thesis may seem foggy even very late in the writing process. Keep writing and revising until the fog lifts.

CHAPTER TWO
Topic to Thesis

Part One: The Topic

The first step in writing the essay is finding a topic. Sometimes this is not difficult: the instructor sets the topic for you, and says, "Three thousand words before Thanksgiving, please." Other times, you must find your own topic, or narrow a very broad topic, such as "Modern Warfare," into one of more manageable scope, such as "Guerrilla Warfare in Central America since the Bay of Pigs Invasion." The topic (from the Greek *topos*) is the "place" you choose to explore in the essay, however you arrive at it. It is the broad field of interest on which you are going to base your research and, hence, your essay.

Choosing a Topic

If a topic has not been assigned by your instructor, be sure to set aside enough time to search for one in the course material. It is wise to determine early in a course how many essays you will be expected to write, whether the topics will be supplied, and if not, what restrictions there are on your choice of topic. The first week of classes is not too early to be thinking about essays you will write. When you enroll in a university course, you will have set, no doubt, certain goals for yourself based upon your interests and career plans. Keep these personal goals in mind while looking for topics of particular interest to you which are, also, central to the course you are studying. A good topic is the beginning of every good essay; therefore, select your topic with care.

What are the essentials of a good topic?

1. ***The topic interests you.*** You will write more effectively about a subject that engages you intellectually and emotionally. If your topic encompasses a probing question or an issue needing to be resolved, you will be able to generate a thesis or develop an argument more easily.

2. ***It is challenging.*** Remember that your essay will differ from others on the basis of interpretations which you develop, lines of investigation which you pursue and connections you make. Topics which allow only for restating someone else's research will not be flexible enough to explore in your own way. For instance, a professor may ask you to discuss B.F. Skinner's approach to behavioural psychology. The task, then, is informed by the word "discuss." If you sketch the system of Skinner's thought but offer no critique, you produce a description. A more appropriate reading of the term "discuss" would lead you not only to sketch his system, but also to assess its influence. Research for your essay should be rewarding; it should add to your store of knowledge. If the material available is old familiar territory, find a more challenging topic to explore. Finally, do not re-submit one of your papers that has received a grade in another course. The reasons are obvious: no new research has been done and your efforts have already been marked and rewarded.

3. ***It has enough scope.*** To return to the topic-as-place analogy, is the topic big enough or complex enough to spend two weeks exploring? Or would you end up moping around the same tourist traps on every page in order to fill the required number of words? On the other hand, it should not be too broad. Try to develop a sixth sense for the "fit" of a topic: its appropriateness to the projected length of the essay and to the course objectives. Eagerness to include everything read or heard about a topic often tempts a student to select one that is so wide-ranging that a focused attempt to penetrate below the surface level is impossible. Very broad topics cannot become very deep in the limited space of an essay. An essay is meant to be an in-depth investigation of a topic, not a survey of vast areas of knowledge.

Sometimes a topic is so intriguing that research for it can go on and on. Try to discipline yourself to fit the task to the time allowed. If you find that a broad, unfocused topic is squandering your time, and all your attempts at focusing it fail, leave it and choose another.

Consider this topic: "The concept of 'the state' has been problematic since the time of the classical Greeks, and by examining the history of the state from 500 B.C. to the present we can arrive at an understanding of its importance." Such a topic is much too broad for an essay; this sort of exploration is akin to the tourist-in-a-hurry mentality parodied in the seventies film, *If It's Tuesday, This Must Be Belgium.* By trying to cover the world, we miss the significance of the "places" we travel through.

4. *Adequate research material is available.* An essay should not require data which you do not have and cannot get. Avoid subjects requiring information that is too specialized, too recent to be substantiated, or too geographically removed for you to find. If the required material is likely to be in another language, make sure that you have the skills to translate your material. Check the library's holdings *before* you commit yourself to a topic. Even a big university library cannot satisfy the research requirements of all topics.

5. *It is directed toward the appropriate audience.* A well-chosen topic will engage the interest and the intellect of instructor and fellow students alike; that is, it will appeal to readers who possess a scholarly level of understanding.

Narrowing the Topic

Sometimes instructors supply only the most general of topics – "modern American poetry"; "organized labour"; "medieval history of Britain"; "human anatomy" – and ask the student to narrow the subject down to appropriate size. To do this you must be mindful of several things: the level of detail at which the course is pitched, the topic's significance within the context of the course, and the projected length of the essay. When an instructor assigns a general topic, it is often done with the hope that the student will find a suitable subtopic to investigate. If you are at all uncertain of the acceptability of the topic you settle on, check with the instructor. This advice applies to choosing your own topic as well.

It may be helpful to consult reference tools to see how the subject has been divided by other writers: [1]

1. The table of contents and the index in a book on the topic can provide good ideas.

---

[1] For more information, see Chapter Three on library research.

2. The library catalogue system will suggest the natural divisions of broad topics and progressively smaller subtopics, and tell you what books the library actually has. There will be a set of volumes located in the catalogue section of the library that lists all the subject headings used in the particular cataloguing system, with subdivisions and cross-reference headings.

3. Journals in the discipline, and indexes to those journals, will indicate what topics others have found interesting and suitable for essay form.

4. Books in the reference section of the library, both general encyclopaedias and reference books for a particular discipline, may help you find a topic of interest.

Most important, though, is your own analysis of the topic. Ask yourself a series of questions about the broad topic to reduce it step by step to a manageable size. Look for the stage at which you feel that the topic is neither so broad that it would result in a shallow essay, nor so narrow that it does not catch enough material in its net to develop an adequate thesis.

Examples of Narrowed Topics

The first three examples are based on the sample essays found in Appendix D.

Political interest groups
    (what are they? how do they work? where?)
        Political interest groups in Canada and the United States
            (differences? similarities? are they successful? why? why not?)
                Interest groups in Canada and the United States: a comparative study

Pathogenic microorganisms
    (which microorganisms? all? too broad)
        Pathogenic viruses
            (characteristics? in humans? in animals?)
                Pathogenic viruses in animals
                    (which animals?)
                        The pathogenesis of viruses and its effects on harbour seals

T.S. Eliot's poetry
  (all of his poetry? too broad)
    T.S. Eliot's *The Waste Land*
    (the whole poem?)
      The final section of T.S. Eliot's *The Waste Land*
        (image patterns? relation to earlier sections?)
          Image patterns in the final section of T.S. Eliot's
          The Waste Land
            (all the very complex imagery? all the patterns?)
              The title image as the centre of the final
              section of T.S. Eliot's *The Waste Land*.

Ecology
    Ecological damage
     (in what way? what kind?)
      Ecological damage resulting from fishing
        (where?)
      Ecological damage resulting from fishing in the
      Otonabee River
        (when?)
          Ecological damage resulting from fishing in the
          Otonabee River during spawning season

(This one can probably not be narrowed much further without becoming too minute.)

Exercise One: Narrowing the Topic

Narrow the following topics. Be aware of the questions you formulate to arrive at each level. What is the length of the essay you have in mind? Afterwards, think about what made you decide to stop narrowing when you did. Does the narrowed topic fulfill the requirements of the original broad topic?

1. The Constitutional Rights of Native People
2. The French Revolution
3. Existentialism
4. Bird Migration

Analyzing the Topic

For many well-intentioned students, the first response to a topic either set by an instructor or chosen by themselves is to race to the library, assignment sheet in hand (or worse, at home) and fill their satchels with whatever books seem somehow relevant. These students hope that if they read around the topic long enough, clarity will emerge. Research is beneficial at this stage, but before you go too far into your topic, some focusing of your chosen purpose is essential.

Once the topic is narrowed, the next task is to determine exactly what the topic chosen (or assigned) requires you to do. Only then can you really begin thinking about what *you* want to do. If you write a brilliant essay on the nesting habits of the great horned owl when you were asked to discuss the mating habits of said bird, you will come to grief at evaluation time.

As soon as you choose or are given a topic, start thinking about the precise nature of the task at hand. Instructors design questions with great care, and expect you to notice every aspect of the question you choose: its wording, its emphasis, its inherent structure. Look for the subject of the topic sentence, the articles and phrases that modify nouns, and the verbs that will direct your research action: search for the meaning of the topic. In every case, your aim should be to focus the topic as best you can before going to the library. To "focus the topic" means to see it as a whole and to determine its main or essential points. Focusing requires you to see the topic as a single subject area and also to see the parts that make the whole clear, logical, and understandable. Remember that you need to take control of the essay process early on if you are not to be overwhelmed by unrelated information. The more focused the topic, the more productive your research work will be.

"Analyze" is from the Greek word meaning "to break up." To analyze your topic means, then, to break it up very carefully into its parts so that you can see it more clearly. This is akin to the process secondary school students bitterly describe as dissecting a poem and thereby taking the life out of it. Neither a poem nor an essay topic is a science-class frog. If you are careful enough in your analysis, you will be able not only to dissect the topic but to put it back together again, to reassemble it, and to begin to create your essay. You will, in effect, be breathing life back into the topic.

Methods of Analysis

Since topics vary in form, they lend themselves to different methods of analysis. Listed below are several approaches.

1. If the topic is not already in the form of a question, *recast the topic in question form*, specifically, in the form of a central question your essay will investigate. Sometimes you can formulate this question very early on; sometimes your preliminary reading will help you find the critical point. Here is an example of how this works. Suppose the topic is:

   > The major cause of student unrest in West Germany is the threat of nuclear war. Discuss.

   One possible question could be:

   > To what extent is the threat of nuclear war the main cause of student unrest in West Germany?

2. *Restate the topic in your own words* to make sure that you understand it. The language that makes deepest sense to you is the language that comes more or less naturally to you. Be careful, though, not to distort or diminish the topic in the translation.

3. *Make sure you understand all the key words and concepts in the question.* Each discipline coins its own words and phrases for concepts that cannot be specifically and unambiguously expressed by an existing word. These are words like "hegemony," "onomatopoeia," "theodicy," and "structuralism," none of which are likely to pass human lips outside of academic circles. Such words are referred to alternately as "jargon," meaning unintelligible sounds that emerge from low in the throat, or as "terminology," meaning the system of words that stakes out the milestones and boundaries (*terminus*) of a discipline.

   In addition, all disciplines employ certain common words in very specialized ways, and it is necessary to be aware of the precise meaning each course assigns to a particular word. For example, consider "class" in biology, "organism" in psychology, "scene" in English, "material" in philosophy, "myth" in anthropology. If you use a dictionary frequently (and you should) you will have noticed that many entries have alternate definitions, some of them keyed to different disciplines, such as medicine, law, or music. You may have to consult specialized reference books such as the *Dictionary of*

Terms or course texts to clarify some words and concepts adequately.

See the glossary at the end of this book for definitions of terms commonly used in essay questions, such as "discuss," "evaluate," and "illustrate." By analyzing these familiar words, you may find the way to begin to interpret the topic.

4. ***Break the topic up into subtopics.*** This approach is a godsend for those eighty-five word lump-like topics that end with the word "discuss." Sometimes such questions begin with the main idea, sometimes the main idea is buried somewhere else in the question, and sometimes the student is expected to deduce the main idea from a series of smaller related ideas. Try rearranging to connect related ideas. Often it is useful to start by copying the question down, beginning a new line for every new sentence. A word of caution here: many students assume that their essays must discuss the ideas presented in the order in which they appear in the question. Not true, and very often not even advisable. Instructors sometimes assign long, complex topics to act as a guide to the several concerns the essay should cover.

The four techniques of analyzing a topic discussed so far direct you toward a full understanding of the *"topos"* or place to be explored. The following three techniques move you right into your essay. The process requires a little imagination. This is the point when you begin to assemble your ideas and make the exact connection between the required task and what is to become your paper.

5. ***Try to picture what some or all of the sections might be.*** Sit quietly and think about your topic. How will you begin? How will you develop your points? Do you see three major sections, maybe five? Do you see subsections emerging? Conceive the form and contemplate the content of your essay.

6. If you have been asked to agree or disagree with a statement, ***try to imagine different positions that might be taken***. This thinking process is an important part of all critical analysis. Try constructing lines of argument by which you can defend those positions. Devise a number of possible approaches to your task; mental elbow-room can rescue you from the temptation to commit yourself to the first approach that comes to mind. The urge to make up one's mind too fast is poisonous to the inquiring intellect. Another very good reason for trying to imagine different positions on a subject is that no matter what position you decide to defend (and you must choose eventually),

you will need to know the contrary points of view in order to convince your reader that your argument stands up to apparently and genuinely opposing evidence.

7. *Try brainstorming.* At this stage, you will want to explore your personal store of knowledge of your topic. You may think you know nothing, but you have, in fact, already done some preliminary research. Try to recall information from your notes, lectures, and tutorials. Often you will be surprised by what will turn up. Sometimes writing down all the specific ideas that come to mind will take you more deeply into your topic. Afterwards, cull the list, throwing out clearly bird-brained ideas. Look for related ideas that you might cluster together. Then be selective: it is unlikely that everything you have in your list belongs in the same essay. Remember that you cannot do everything in one paper, and for every topic many different and equally appropriate essays are possible.

Checklist: Analyzing the Topic
1. **Recast the topic in question form.**
2. **Restate the topic in your own words.**
3. **Make sure that you understand all the key words and concepts.**
4. **Break the topic up into a set of smaller parts.**
5. **Picture what some or all of the sections of your essay might be.**
6. **Imagine different positions.**
7. **Brainstorm.**

If you have made a noble attempt to analyze the topic, but you are still feeling a bit uncertain of its precise meaning, ask your instructor for advice. Most instructors are pleased to assist students who are working hard. Finally, remember that some topics are not as well-phrased as they might be, and no amount of analysis will wring clarity from an inherently ambiguous or illogical sentence. Again, ask your instructor for assistance in interpreting the topic. Sometimes you have a better grasp on the topic than you think, and just talking about it allows you to see it more clearly.

Exercise Two: Recasting the Topic in Question Form

What questions suggested by these topics might serve as the central inquiry of an essay?

1. World War I and its impact on the Maritime Provinces.

2. The status of Irish immigrants in the United States during the nineteenth century.

3. The locomotive systems of the ant and the fly.

4. Love and fancy in *A Midsummer Night's Dream.*

5. Canada's environmental policies and ozone depletion.

Exercise Three: Key Words and Concepts

Rephrase the following topics. Then use whatever reference tools are available to find the definitions of the words and concepts used in each question. When you have confidence in the accuracy of your understanding of the topics, rephrase them again. Compare the results with your first attempts.

1. The negative environmental consequences vis-à-vis the economic advantages of the implementation of advanced technology. [Course in World Development]

2. The commodification of virtue in the modern world. [Course in Sociology of the Workplace]

3. The Treaty of Westphalia (1648) ended the Thirty Years' War and also ended the religious conflicts brought about by the Reformation and Counter-Reformation. [Course in European History]

4. Compare the methodological approach of Creighton in his analysis of Canadian settlement patterns with that of Harold Innis in his staples thesis. [Course in Canadian Studies]

5. *Waiting for Godot* bespeaks a world view less witty and a thematic reach less ambitious than many plays from the theatre of the absurd. What then accounts for its time-proven power to elicit the affection and attention of theatre audiences? [Course in Modern Drama]

Exercise Four: Subdividing the Topic

Read the following topics. Analyze each question and decide whether all parts are of equal importance, and if not, which parts should receive more emphasis than others. Are some parts subsections of other parts? What is the overall point of each question? Finish by rewriting the questions, beginning with a statement of the main idea of each.

1. The economic system in Canada that brought about the prosperous 50s and 60s now appears to leave us only the alternatives of high inflation or massive unemployment. Must we have one or the other? Does full employment mean that we must suffer insidious inflation? Is the capitalist system structurally flawed? Would a mixed economy offer a genuine solution to our problems, or only disguise them?

2. Discuss the social effects of the Industrial Revolution in Britain. How did the society of the Industrial Revolution differ from that which preceded it? Did technological advances change the way people saw their world? Did the new economic arrangements affect interpersonal relations? To what extent does our own society perpetuate the patterns which were established during the Industrial Revolution?

Exercise Five: Breaking Up the Topic

What sections and subsections are suggested by the following topics?

1. Describe and explain the changes in spatial patterns of population in Canada since 1945, and indicate how these changes have affected Canadian cities.

2. Examine the struggles of French Canada for a separate cultural and political identity from that of the rest of Canada during the period of The Quiet Revolution. Refer to incidents of both violence and cooperation.

Exercise Six: Finding a Position

Imagine different positions that you could take on the following topics:

1. Discuss the comparative strengths and limitations of solar and nuclear energy in terms of cost and environmental safety.

2. Are AIDS hospices necessary in Ontario? Discuss.

Exercise Seven: Brainstorming

Spend five minutes jotting down everything that comes to mind on the following topics. Then cull the list and group related ideas.

1. Differences in the capabilities of men and women in professional sports result entirely from unequal training. Discuss.

2. "The twentieth century has seen poetry decline in popularity while the short story has become a more preferred literary genre." Is this true? Why? Why not?

Part Two: The Thesis

Generating a Thesis

Once you have focused a topic by narrowing it sufficiently and analyzing its component parts, you will be ready to begin looking for a thesis. If the topic can be thought of as the area to be explored, the thesis is the purpose you aim to fulfill when you reach your destination. Every academic essay must have such a purpose: not necessarily an argument *per se,* but a central insight or proposition or explication that captures what you consider to be the most important results of your thinking.

Does every essay, then, have a "thesis"?

Yes. But it is not always an explicit and identifiable statement. Sometimes the thesis is the general controlling idea that provides overall unity and direction to your essay. Therefore, every essay has a thesis even though not every essay has a thesis statement.

In some disciplines a description may be required in a paper; the students will be asked to do some research, read journal articles or scholarly books, and restate, in their own words, the themes and concepts covered by the authors of these secondary materials. On other occasions, they may be asked to do a précis, an abstract, or a prose summary of experimental data. These forms of writing still need to follow formal principles of organization and they are still a mirror of the thought processes of the writer. And, even though the writer is not confronted with the mystery of an innovative writing task, even though the introduction, body, and conclusion of the piece are all known at the outset, the organization and presentation are still an expression of personality, of mind, emotion, and soul. One might sit down to describe the mechanics of a hydraulic lock, or the culture of the Mohawk Indian, or the anatomy of a praying mantis, and in each instance there is little or no room for original insights; the research calls only for the retrieval of well-documented facts from the library. Yet in organizing that material, and in rendering it into prose, the choice of word and phrase, and the decision of where to begin and end will all be acts of personal imagination and intellect. All this is just a complex way of saying that no integrated body of writing can exist (that is, communicate with its reader) unless it expresses the self-conscious designs of its author. An essay may not require a thesis statement, but it does need to have a principle of organization, some generative and cohesive force to shape, form, and interconnect its sentences. If we define a "thesis" as the sustained purpose, the *raison d'être* of the writing task, then we would say, "Yes, every essay has a thesis because every essay contains the self-conscious purpose of its writer at every stage of its creation."

Whatever your discipline, the thesis is your way into a topic. A topic alone cannot lead you into any kind of academic essay. A topic is merely the terrain you need to keep in view: it is neutral, flat, without intellectual value until an inquiring mind has established a purpose for exploring it. Again, consider the original meaning of the two words, both from classical Greek:

topic = *topos,* "place"
thesis = "something set down"

A thesis is something declared, a decision made, a direction found. In its ideal formulation, it is the essayist's crystal-clear apprehension of purpose that acts as gravitational centre and navigational device throughout the course of writing the essay.

At this stage of thinking through your essay, it might be helpful to visualize the process as a series of loosely formed circles. Each circle evolves from the whole; each forms a relationship with the other:

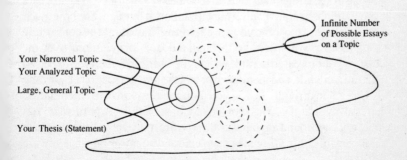

Infinite Number of Possible Essays on a Topic

Your Narrowed Topic
Your Analyzed Topic
Large, General Topic

Your Thesis (Statement)

In the following examples, the topic outlines the subject to be covered, and the thesis declares the position the writer has taken.

Examples:

Topic: The Viet Nam War
Narrowed Topic: American involvement in the Viet Nam War.
Analyzed Topic: What was the most important cause of America's increased involvement in the Viet Nam War during the 60s?

Thesis: The escalation of the Viet Nam War during the 60s was caused primarily by America's anti-Communist foreign policy.

Topic: Virginia Woolf's *To The Lighthouse*.
Narrowed Topic: The last chapter of *To The Lighthouse*.
Analyzed Topic: What are the major themes? How are these developed? By imagery, especially in the last chapter.

Thesis: The major themes of *To The Lighthouse* are resolved in the imagery of its last chapter.

Searching for a Thesis

While you are unlikely to know your exact thesis until you have done more reading and possibly begun writing, you should try to approximate it as soon as you can. The process of essay writing is very much a matter of probing ahead at each stage, whether trying to picture the shape of the essay or anticipating what conclusions your investigations are pointing toward. From the earliest stages of the experience, you should be trying to see farther than you can see clearly. When a vivid idea occurs to you (it might be at first only a hunch), follow it through. See how much sense it makes of the topic you are exploring. You might be completely wrong at first; you might go through a dozen formulations over the course of your research period; you might find a bird when you expected to find an aardvark, and then discover that the bird is a sandpiper standing up close when through the fog you thought it was an ostrich a hundred metres away. But if you had not looked for something in particular, you would not have found anything at all. You are much more likely to locate that powerful controlling idea that accurately centres on what you are discovering if you are always looking for it than if you are not. In the course of careful, attentive, and always-ready-to-be-fooled prediction, we probe toward, and ultimately see, exactly what is there.

It is a big mistake to defer thinking deeply about your thesis until all your research is done. Research in this sense is really *search,* a search to find relevant material and make connections. Finding a thesis is a recursive process that begins the moment we embark on a new course of study. Blinding and sudden revelations do occur in academic work, but they are not to be counted on. If you jump into your research and allow yourself to go off in all directions without any idea of what your thesis might be, you increase the chances of wasting time reading material that turns out to be irrelevant. Worse, you could so confuse yourself with undirected information that any possibility of a central organizing idea emerging from the chaos is lost. It is in such cauldrons of conscientiously achieved disarray that the more peculiar and painfully awkward essays are brewed. "All hope abandon, ye who enter here."[2]

The question remains, how exactly do I find this lodestone around which all my ideas will adhere in cosmic harmony? It makes sense to begin by thinking about the topic. For example, if you are asked whether the debate about the morality of slavery or economic conditions contributed more significantly to the American Civil War, your thesis will present your opinion of the primary causes of the war and an indication of the reasons for your belief. No doubt you will want to define the various causes as contributing, necessary, or sufficient. Give yourself time to mull over ideas and to imagine how things fit together. Above all, as you generate your thesis, pay attention to any particular aspect of your material that seems of paramount interest and importance to you. You will have little trouble identifying your thesis once you locate a compelling focus.

You will want to decide what kind of essay best suits your subject and your assignment. Will it be necessary to persuade your reader about a controversial point? Do you want to describe something by supplying substantial and convincing data? Or is your purpose to explain something by weighing several different points of view? As you come closer to the point you want to make, the method by which you will be communicating it to your reader will form.

---

[2]Dante Alighieri, "Inferno," *The Divine Comedy,* III.ix, quoted in *Dictionary of Quotations*, ed. Bergen Evans (New York: Avenel, 1978) 165.

Asking Questions to Find the Thesis

If you have done some reading and are still having trouble finding a thesis, try asking the following questions about your material:

1. *Why?*
   Does your material lend itself to answering a "why" question? Why did the event take place; why were these conditions present? For example, you might explain why Japanese Canadians were so harshly treated during World War II.

2. *How?*
   Could your material provide an answer to a "how" question? Could you explain how a particular cultural practice evolved, or how a bee communicates with other members of its hive, or how decisions are made in the White House?

3. *What?*
   Can you ask what role a historical or fictional figure played in events, what the most important aspect of a theory is, what the function of a specific image is in the work of literature you are studying? For example, you might ask what Lester Pearson's most important contribution to foreign affairs was, or what the green light symbolizes in F. Scott Fitzgerald's novel *The Great Gatsby*. Only be careful that your "what" questions are not simplistic. A university essay should not catalogue historical events or summarize the plot of a novel, which a question like "What happened?" would invite you to do. Your "what" questions should lead you to explain, interpret, or define: not "What people watch television evangelists?" but "What accounts for the popularity of television evangelists?" Useful "what" questions can normally be rephrased into "why" or "how" questions.

Get into the habit of asking all kinds of questions when you are looking for a way into your material. By posing and answering significant questions, you should be able to identify an important and interesting thesis.

These general questions – why, how, what, and what if – might lead you to more specific inquiries about your material. Listed below are some approaches you might try:

1. *Cause*
   Are the causes of an event or a process of particular importance? You might look at the causes of an historical event, a sociological

phenomenon, or a particular disease. Are the causes contributing, necessary, or sufficient?

2. *Effect*
   In looking at your material, can you ascertain important effects or results? For example, what has been the effect of the introduction of oral rehydration therapy in developing countries? Has the lowering of the drinking age resulted in an increase in automobile deaths in the 18-21 age group?

3. *Comparison*
   Does a comparison of certain aspects of your material interest you? Could you compare two theories of chivalry, the humorous techniques of Leacock and Twain, or two sources of electrical power?

4. *Strengths and Weaknesses*
   Can you examine the strengths and weaknesses of a theory, a politician, a play? For example, you might consider the strengths and weaknesses of the political policies of the late Ayatollah Khomaini, or of Margaret Atwood's argument that the central theme of Canadian literature is survival.

5. *Pros and Cons*
   Does your material lend itself to an examination of pros and cons? For example, what are the pros and cons of Canada's deploying a fleet of nuclear-powered submarines in the Arctic or of chemical and organic fertilizers?

6. *Chronological Development*
   Can you trace a development in your material? You might look at the development of a character in a novel, a symbol throughout a poet's works, the evolution of primates, or the transition of a dictatorship to a democracy. Chronology (the development through time) of your material could be its most interesting aspect. For instance, you might argue that Coleridge's awareness of the unconscious and its relation to creativity predated that of both Freud and Jung. Be careful, however. A chronological approach can easily degenerate into a mere recitation of facts and dates with no relevant interpretation of material. Skillfully handled, though, the approach can be interesting, especially when significant connections are made.

Remember that a good thesis:
a) **answers the question or fulfills the assignment set by the instructor, and**
b) **presents the argument that seems most significant and most interesting to you.**

The Thesis Statement

Through the process of critical inquiry and research, the writer moves in the direction of transforming topics into theses, and in most cases, into thesis statements. A strong thesis statement or a strong sense of purpose can make the difference between a rambling essay that seems to circle around the point without ever finding it (or, almost worse, the Five-&-Dime-catalogue sort of essay – the one that contains an arrangement of a little bit of everything), and an essay with a lively forward impetus that proceeds with deliberate purpose. A carefully chosen thesis statement can prevent both befuddled wandering and mechanical, superficial development. It can do all this, of course, only if you make proper use of it. Even if your thesis does not take the form of a statement, your writing should, with every sentence, convey a sense of purpose to the reader.

You should keep this sense of purpose in mind while you are preparing your outline, doing your research, writing your essay, riding the bus. If it is in the form of a statement, it serves both as centre of gravity and homing device. A clear and succinct statement of your central idea helps you to notice subtle aspects of your topic that support or undermine your purpose. As you toil through a particularly difficult passage, remaining aware of your thesis statement will help you to remain true to the general direction you have set for your paper.

In order to work this way, the thesis must be just right. The purpose you have in mind should be formed sufficiently to be completely integrated with the topic you have chosen. A thesis statement must be short enough (probably one sentence) that you can keep the entire statement in mind as a single object of contemplation. It cannot serve as a useful compass if it points in more than one direction. To get the thesis to a useful stage, you may well have to go through many formulations of it over the course of your preparation for the essay. You may finally find it only by beginning the essay, and once you have written your way into realizing what your thesis is, by starting your paper again. But a good thesis statement is worth the effort. Do not mistake a feeling of familiarity with the subject for an awareness of purpose. Sometimes thoughts must be put to the test of words, submitted to the constraints of strict syntax, before we can see illogicalities and foggy patches. It is, after all, the grand claim, distinction, and hope of the university that by careful thinking we can know things more deeply, in more complexity, and therefore more accurately than without.

Writing the Thesis Statement

The thesis statement, then, declares the controlling idea of the essay: it states the purpose of the essay and indicates the design by which that purpose will be fulfilled. The thesis statement should be a proposition, not a question or a topic. Remember, it is something set down, an assertion or position statement. Because it is a rather large something, it cannot be an isolated detail of the larger question; it must be sufficient and general enough to cover the topic. Consider, for example, the difference between the following topic, question arising from the topic, and thesis statement:

Topic: Diefenbaker and the Cuban missile crisis.
Question: What were the results of Diefenbaker's response to the Cuban
            missile crisis?
Thesis Statement:
            Diefenbaker's indecisiveness during the Cuban missile
            crisis not only damaged his chances of reelection, but also
            hurt Canada's image abroad.

In this example, the topic is focused on a general area of study, the question indicates the critical point the writer has selected, the thesis declares the argument the writer will develop. The specifics — incidents of Diefenbaker's indecisiveness, the ways in which these affected his chances of reelection, and Canada's image abroad — will become the material to be covered within the essay.

Thesis statements do not need to be controversial: you may often write a thesis statement with which anyone conversant with the subject would agree. And originality, in the sense of an approach never before committed to paper in the history of academia, is not required before the PhD dissertation. However, good thesis statements are never self-evidently true. Rather, they need the support of the evidence, details, and examples which a thorough consideration of the subject reveals.

The thesis statement may appear in the introduction to your essay or in the conclusion. Often the introduction is the more useful place for it; a statement of your central proposition at the beginning of your essay will enable your reader to see the direction in which the essay is moving. Besides, essays are not mystery novels, and unless you are a master of the technique, you are likely to irritate and confuse your reader by tucking the thesis in the middle of your essay or withholding it until the end. In any case, remember that while the thesis statement is helpful to your reader, its primary purpose in life is to help you. No matter where it makes its first appearance in your essay, it should at all times be in your mind.

Complex Thesis Statements

Interesting, well-conceived thesis statements often declare an apparent contradiction. Such theses can be productive of complex, penetrating insights into your material. There are several reasons for this.

First, by its very nature the process of exploring a contradiction requires you to notice the similarities and differences between things, and often we can see something best by defining it not only in terms of what it is but in terms of what it is not.

Second, academic work is aimed above all at discovering the actual nature of things, whether the precise movements of a poem, or the internal chemistry of the DNA molecule, or the specific psychological impulses behind the consumer's choice of a brand name item. And the actual nature of things, we keep discovering, is complex and contradictory: people can behave like monsters or saints and still be human beings, for example. The compelling quality of much of the world's most powerful literature derives in part from its exploration of some deep contradiction or paradox or irony or tension between opposing forces at the heart of human life. Greek tragedy and English Romantic poetry are two examples, the former obsessed with the gulf between intention and result, the latter with the tension between our constitutional tendency toward apathy and our constitutional capacity for joy.

The complex thesis statement is preferable to the simple one, then, for at least two reasons: it challenges you to analyze your subject more precisely, and it is often a better reflection of the reality of things. In any case, it is disastrous to pretend that something complex can be made simple by loading all the evidence on one side.

A good thesis statement, remember, can propel you through your essay, but only if it declares a sufficiently energetic idea. A statement that holds two contradictory elements in tension usually has the required energy. The tension might be in a contrast between your own and the traditional interpretation of an historical event or literary work, between appearance or reputation and reality, and so on. If you are having trouble finding a thesis, try formulating one that begins with "although." If you set yourself a challenging task at the thesis stage, you will find that you have done yourself a favour when you come to write the essay.

Checklist: Thesis Statements

1. **Does your thesis statement do more than restate the topic or question?** It should present the results of your investigation, not announce your intention to investigate. This thesis statement declares an intention:

   > This essay will examine the effects of gamma-rays on man-in-the-moon marigolds.

   This preferred thesis statement indicates the results of a study:

   > Gamma-rays cause strange mutations of man-in-the-moon marigolds.

2. **Does your thesis statement reflect the restrictions which your essay will impose on the subject?** For example this thesis statement does not tell the reader the limits imposed on the main point to be discussed:

   > Work exploits people instead of freeing them.

   This preferred thesis statement defines the restrictions:

   > The prosperity of investors in twentieth century Britain depends on the maintenance of a large labour pool of people who work for minimum wage.

3. **Is your thesis statement written clearly so that it states the central idea of your essay precisely?** This thesis statement is imprecise and unclear:

   > It is hard to say what ever became of Quebec's spirit; the issue has remained unresolved after years of debate.

   This preferred statement indicates the writer's argument:

   > Quebec nationalism is not dead; it is merely dormant.

4. **Does your thesis statement convey the priorities of your argument?** You should give your reader a clear expectation of how your argument will develop and which ideas are most important. This statement does not tell the reader what the writer considers to be the key point:

> The stalemate at Rekjavik was a real set-back for nuclear disarmament and it is difficult to see if any progress was made at the Icelandic summit.

This preferred statement indicates the writer's priorities:

> Although the Rekjavik talks ended in stalemate, the cause for disarmament was furthered at the Icelandic summit.

5. **Is your thesis statement brief, written preferably in one and no more than two sentences?**

6. **Does your thesis statement present a proposition which can be proven?** Avoid statements that are narrowly factual, overly subjective, illogical or sensational. Consider this statement:

> Einstein was the greatest physicist of all time. All of his theories were, and continue to be, foolproof.

This is too much to be proven in a single essay. It would be better to evaluate carefully one of his theories stressing its merits and indicating how it has stood the test of time.

7. **So what?** If you ask this of your thesis statement and nothing comes to mind, your thesis statement reveals nothing of significance, or its truth is too readily apparent. You want your reader to be intellectually responsive to the material you cover and the meaning you create.

Exercise Eight: Topic to Thesis Statement

Propose a thesis for each of the several hypothetical topics listed below. Do not be too concerned about whether the statement made is right or wrong, accurate or ill-informed. The important thing for the purpose of this exercise is to make a clear, strong statement of your position on the topic.

1. The role of the narrator in *Heart of Darkness*.

2. Assess the impact of television, video games, and rock videos on an individual growing up in the electronic age.

3. Is state censorship justifiable in the case of hate propaganda and violent pornography?

4. The relations between francophone and anglophone Canadians in the eighties.

5. Should the principal purpose of environmentalists be to correct the problems technology creates? Should environmentalists be proactive as well as reactive? If they are proactive, are they not seeking to dominate and control nature in much the same manner as industrial technology does?

Exercise Nine: Sample Thesis Statements

In the space provided, indicate whether each thesis statement below is good or poor. In the case of a poor thesis statement, indicate by number which of the criteria on the thesis statement checklist it fails to meet. If you have time, explain your evaluation and propose a better version.

_____ 1. This essay will examine the effects of prohibiting fishing in the Otonabee River during spawning season.

_____ 2. The development of steel was very important in the growth of a distinctively new architecture both in Europe and in North America.

_____ 3. Every socioeconomic group in North America has suffered adverse effects from the growth of technology in the twentieth century.

_____ 4. Both in terms of major energy production, such as the generation of electricity for cities, and in terms of localized energy needs, such as the fuel for a single automobile, hydrogen is the source of power of the future.

_____ 5. Shakespeare's _King Lear_ is pervaded by images of animals, of torture, and of clothing.

_____ 6. When Prime Minister Pierre Trudeau reluctantly invoked the War Measures Act in October, 1970, he was courageously defending his citizens from the imminent loss of their freedoms at the hands of the lunatic fringe.

_____ 7. Food processing is not detrimental to the value of the food itself. When we look at nature we see that nuts and seeds are preserved to last over several winters, and honey is really refined sugar.

_____ 8. Like many animals, bees can communicate with one another. Bees that have found nectar will return to the hive. There they perform dance-like motions. These motions can communicate information about direction and distance.

_____ 9. Although Canada's anti-Jewish immigration policy during the Holocaust has been blamed on the prejudice of a few officials, the main reason for its adoption can be found in Mackenzie King's sensitivity to the political climate of his country: anti-Semitism was a vote-getter.

_____ 10. Although Marx debunked religion as "the opiate of the people," the structure of his thought is deeply theological.

_____ 11. Life and death are exchanges, not ends.

_____ 12. It is no longer the case that the city wastes and the farm conserves: agricultural pollution is posing a considerable threat to the environment. With a diminishing amount of land on which to farm and with heavier use of that land, agri-businesses are heading toward an ecological crisis.

_____ 13. Capital expenditure for business is earmarked to 1995.

_____ 14. Although one is a high-spirited comedy and the other a brutal tragedy, the Medieval plays of "The Nativity" and "The Crucifixion" explore a common theme: the intersection of the human and the divine.

_____ 15. The younger generation is more aware of the need to protect the environment and trim its lifestyle than the older.

_____ 16. There are those who claim that while man is the pinnacle of land-evolved animals, whales are at the top of the evolutionary scale in the oceans. Has man, on this planet, an evolutionary equal in the whale?

_____ 17. The prison in the novel demonstrates how its characters are caged mentally and live frustrated lives.

CHAPTER THREE
Research

Although not all essays are research essays, all essays require research. Research begins as soon as you consult someone or something outside of yourself, and it usually goes on until you have written and revised the last word of your essay. Even if you consult only one external source, a work of literature for example, you are still researching.

Research can be defined as a close searching, a studious, critical investigation of a well-defined topic. The word is derived from the Latin word *circare* which means "to go round." This is essentially what you do when you research a topic; you try to encircle it, to mark its boundaries. You progress to the subject's core in an ever-tightening spiral. Research helps you focus your topic, formulate and refine your thesis, and discover details, opinions and facts against which you can test this thesis.

Because most people are curious, research can become a monster of voracious appetite; it can swell so large that unbridled it will eat all your time, and will attempt to eat New York even though your essay topic is Fifth Avenue. You therefore need to take control of the research process from the beginning. Your interests and the demands of your topic and thesis direct your research; the time you have to prepare an essay and its projected length limit it. By following the steps outlined in this chapter, you will be able to control your hunger for tasty but irrelevant details while assuring that you gather enough substantial information to flesh out your essay.

Beginning

You may need to do preliminary research to find a topic or to refine one. Begin by doing some general reading. There are several good starting places: course syllabi, the required and recommended readings listed in course outlines, textbooks and lecture notes, books and articles dealing with the major themes of your courses. Also useful are the various reference books available in most libraries. Encyclopaedias, biographical dictionaries, chronologies, and handbooks can give you an overview of a particular discipline, subject, or era. They can also give you a sense of the range of possible topics open to you, and a sense of the larger context of any one topic that you might have chosen.

Encyclopaedia articles are particularly useful in preliminary research, even though any professor would be quite rightly horrified to receive a paper for which such an article constituted the main research effort. Most of us know about general encyclopaedias like the *Encyclopedia Americana* or the *New Encyclopedia Britannica,* but there are many specialized encyclopaedias which provide detailed coverage of various academic subjects. These encyclopaedias are full of articles by scholars who are expert in the fields for which they write entries. Some of these specialized encyclopaedias include the *Encyclopedia of Philosophy, The International Encyclopedia of the Social Sciences,* and the *McGraw-Hill Encyclopedia of Science and Technology.*

If your topic is a person, an article in a biographical dictionary could fulfill the same purpose as an article in a specialized encyclopaedia. These dictionaries generally classify famous people by nationality, historical period, or profession. You can find information on scientists in the *Dictionary of Scientific Biography,* and articles on famous governors of Canada, for example, in the *Dictionary of National Biography* (which provides entries on British persons now deceased) and in the *Dictionary of Canadian Biography.* There is even an index to biographical entries in reference works entitled the *Biography and Genealogy Master Index.*

To discover what reference works are available, consult the *Guide to Reference Books* and the library's catalogues. Do not hesitate to seek the assistance of reference librarians. Besides giving good advice, they often have printed research guides designed to assist you in your search.

Choosing Your Research Direction

Once you have decided upon a topic, analyzed this topic, narrowed it appropriately, defined your special approach to it, and formulated a tentative thesis, you still have at least two decisions to make before your major research effort starts. You must decide how much of the topic needs research, and what kind of research is needed.

Some questions cannot be solved by research alone. A moral or a logical problem might not lend itself to research. Consider the following question:

Is capital punishment just?

Your answer to this would depend more upon your beliefs and upon your capacity to justify these beliefs logically than upon your ability to collect and interpret information. Consider the following essay topic, also about capital punishment:

Examine the backgrounds of both the proponents and adversaries of capital punishment in Canada's current government to determine how similar or different their past experiences have been. What do these similarities or differences suggest about the debate over reinstating the death penalty in Canada?

Obviously, this topic requires extensive research.

Once you have determined that your topic requires research, you should think about what kind of research is necessary. What type of information do you need? Can the questions generated by your topic be answered through observation or experimentation? An essay on cadmium uptake in mussels might require both a review of literature on this subject and extensive field work. Perhaps you need to survey opinion or to design and distribute a questionnaire to test the validity of your thesis. Activities such as these require you to generate your own statistical or experimental data.

Also, you should be aware that other useful information might be available outside of the library's walls. You could interview local lawyers and social workers while researching an essay on child abuse in your area, or you might consult a student from Africa before writing an essay on developing countries. Semi-public documents like organization and corporate records might help a student engaged in market research. Trips to various art galleries in Ontario might be necessary for a student writing about Tom Thomson's brush technique. This does not mean that library research is not valuable. In fact, many of the questions generated by a topic can only be answered by consulting the documents, manuscripts, audio-visual material, statistics, maps, periodicals, and books housed within libraries, museums, archives, and other information centres.

Checklist: Choosing Your Research Direction

1. **Can this topic be researched? Can your thesis be supported by discovering facts and how they have been interpreted?** Is your topic too autobiographical or too subjective to demand research? Logic problems or questions based on moral assumptions are generally not answered by collecting information.

2. **Is this topic too restricted, too current, or too broad to be researched effectively?** Sometimes, if a topic is very recent or extremely restrictive, there is not enough information available upon which to base an essay. For example, it would be impossible to assess the full impact of US President Bush's leadership if you were writing in 1989. Alternatively, a very broad topic must be limited by considerations of the amount of time you have to research and write the essay, as well as by your essay's projected length.

3. **Is this topic interesting enough for you to spend time researching it?** If you have a choice, try to select topics that seem significant to you. After all, if you are curious about a topic, you are more likely to spend time researching it, and your research is likely to be more directed.

4. **What kind of research is suggested by your topic and thesis?** Imagine that you are researching the status of women in nineteenth-century Canada. Inherent in this subject are as many different research strategies as there are theses. For example, you might choose to examine what the laws of marriage, divorce, property ownership, and the family were by looking at Canada's statutes. You could try to discover how many women worked outside the home and how women's wages compared to men's by investigating statistical sources of information. You could look at women's diaries of the period to see what various women thought their role and status should be, or determine what status men generally ascribed to women by reading men's literature. Obviously, there are many other directions your research could take in this instance. Whatever your topic, the choice of direction is yours.

5. **How available and how complex is the material that must be consulted?** There is no use deciding to write an essay on how children were portrayed in magazine advertisements of the 1950s if you cannot consult the appropriate magazines. Also, a student attempting to define and contrast various philosophical and scientific theories

of time might find this task too time-consuming because of its complexity.

Exercise One: Choosing Your Research Direction

Use the checklist above to help you think about the following topics. Which topics demand research, and what kind of research might be needed? How should this research be limited, and what problems might the researcher encounter?

1. Describe the occupational hazards faced by workers in nuclear generating stations and assess the nuclear power industry's safety regulations.

2. Michelet, Marx, and Macaulay were all products of eras of rapid and revolutionary change. Examine how their backgrounds influenced their concepts of history.

3. Has the creation of a welfare state in Canada led to a significant redistribution of income and wealth? Why or why not?

4. Examine how popular music both reflects and influences its audience.

5. Should governments be able to prohibit smoking in public places?

6. Alistair MacLeod reveals a certain ambivalence toward the family in his book of short stories *The Lost Salt Gift of Blood*. Discuss the significance of the title of MacLeod's book in relation to his portrayal of the family.

Library Research

As soon as possible, make the time to acquaint yourself with the organization of the library. You will find libraries inviting and comfortable once you know how they are arranged. In fact, most libraries are a little like local pubs or coffee houses; they attract regulars who come to chat, read, and dry their socks on radiators. If your library offers tours, take one. Find out what kinds of catalogues the library provides. Are there separate sections for specialized material such as government documents, maps, rare books, archival material, audio-visual resources, periodicals, and reference books? These materials may have their own catalogues or they may be listed in the main library catalogue. Next, browse through the reference section for each subject you take. All subjects have specialized reference books which you should be aware of, especially if you want to be a Trivial Pursuit champion. There are too many different kinds of reference works to mention here. However, besides the dictionaries and encyclopaedias already discussed, there are concordances, almanacs, chronologies, statistical abstracts, atlases, indexes, abstracts, and bibliographies.

Many times in the course of essay writing you will want to retrieve a specific piece of information, a detail to prove a point or close an argument. For example, you might want to know what the chemical composition of aspirin is or how many Canadian military personnel died in World War I. A familiarity with the reference books in your field will allow you to answer these and similar questions quickly.

Most often, however, you use reference works to produce a "working bibliography" of library material potentially useful to your chosen topic. You must make a broad examination of available and relevant books, articles, and other library resources before evaluating them in order to determine which are most appropriate to your essay. Sometimes the instructor will provide a preliminary bibliography of suggested or required readings, and it is your job to assess this list, tailor it to your particular purpose, and add to it. Your working bibliography should contain more works than you expect to use, because some will turn out not to be useful. To develop your list, use the bibliographies, abstracts, and indexes available in the reference section, and of course, use the library's catalogues.

Library Catalogues
Library catalogues may appear in many different forms. Some are printed and published as bibliographies, some are produced on microfiche sheets, some are computer databases made available through terminals, and others are in the familiar card form. Microfiche and microcomputer catalogues, like card catalogues, list library holdings by author, title, and subject. Microcomputer or online catalogues display catalogue entries on a computer terminal. These terminals are actually quite easy to use. If you have trouble figuring out the various menus presented to you on the computer screen, catch the eye of a passing librarian and ask him or her to explain them to you. Microfiche catalogues store catalogue information on fiches, sturdy transparent film sheets each of which contains photographically-reduced print. Sets of fiches are stored in binders, boxes, or rotating files located near micro-fiche readers which are machines that magnify the print on a viewing

screen. Gradually, card catalogues and printed catalogues are being replaced by microfiche catalogues and online catalogues. Often, libraries will use a combination of forms. They may, for example, have their older holdings listed in a card catalogue and their newer acquisitions listed in a microcatalogue. Discover what the circumstances are at your library.

Although catalogues differ in form and in the cataloguing system they use, they have similarities; they all attempt to organize material logically so that it can be found quickly. Periodicals are usually listed in catalogues by their complete title and by their general subject. Books are listed in catalogues by author, title, and subject. Subjects may consist of a significant or key word taken from the item's title, or they may be selected by a cataloguer from a controlled list of subject headings. Since this last approach is more common, a guide to the subject headings available to cataloguers can assist students in locating pertinent material within catalogues. Two such guides are frequently used in tandem by Canadian academic libraries: *Library of Congress Subject Headings (LCSH)* and *Canadian Subject Headings (CSH)*. The following chart will allow you to decipher *LCSH* and *CSH* so that you can use these tools to select subject headings of relevance.

LCSH

Compulsory military service
USE Draft

Draft   *(May Subd Geog)*
     ₍UB340-UB355₎
     Here are entered works on conscription for service in a country's armed forces.
  UF   Compulsory military service
       Conscription, Military
       Military conscription
       Selective service
       Service, Compulsory military
       Universal military training
  BT   National service
       Recruiting and enlistment
  RT   Conscientious objectors
  SA   *subdivision* Recruiting, enlistment, etc.
       under individual military services,
       e.g. United States.   Army—
       Recruiting, enlistment, etc.
 — Law and legislation   *(May Subd Geog)*
     BT   Military law
 — Great Britain
     NT   Commissions of array

UF (Used for)
Terms listed here are not subject headings. If you look under these terms in LCSH, you would be referred to the correct subject heading by a **USE** reference.

BT (Broader term)
These are broader subject headings.

RT (Related term)
These are related subject headings.

NT (Narrower term)
These are narrower subject headings.

SA (See also)
General information is listed here. For example, an explanation of the use of subdivisions to express the topic under consideration might be undertaken.

CSH

Rail transportation—Canada
   see   Railroads—Canada

Railroads—Canada

> Works about particular railways as transportation systems are entered under topical headings for their conventional names, e.g. **Canadian Pacific Railway.** These headings may vary from, but should match as closely as possible the headings for the corresponding railway companies as corporate bodies, e.g. **Canadian Pacific Railway Company** or **CP Rail.**

  sa   Eminent domain—Canada
         Express service—Canada
         Freight and freightage—Canada
         Subways—Canada
   x   Canada—Railroads
         Rail transportation—Canada
         Railways—Canada
  xx   Transportation—Canada

sa (see also)   This abbreviation precedes references made to subject headings for related or subordinate topics. The words and phrases listed after **sa** are subject headings, and they are generally narrower than the subject heading under which they appear.

x (see from)   This symbol designates references that have been made to the subject heading from expressions not used as subject headings. Since the words and phrases listed after the **x** symbol are not subject headings, there is no point in a researcher looking them up in library catalogues.

xx (see also from)   Following this symbol, there is a record of expressions from which **sa** references have been made to the subject heading. The words and phrases listed after the **xx** symbol are subject headings, and they are generally broader than the subject heading under which they appear.

Armed with a list of headings gleaned from *LCSH* and *CSH,* approach the "Subject" section of the catalogue. The subject headings are arranged alphabetically, and within a subject heading, authors and titles are similarly arranged. If your course bibliography supplies you with authors' names and titles of books on your topic, you might locate these books more quickly by searching the "Author" or "Title" section of the catalogue. In some small libraries, subjects, authors, and titles are all inter-filed alphabetically in one large dictionary catalogue. Most academic libraries, however, do separate their catalogues into two or three distinct sections. Make sure that you don't conduct a fruitless search for a subject heading in the "Title" or "Author" section of the catalogue.

Catalogue entries yield a surprising amount of information, often enough for you to decide whether to look for the catalogued item. Upon finding what seems to be a useful entry, note the bibliographic information given in the catalogue and the call number on an index card. If you take time to do this now, you will avoid the problem of not being able to complete your bibliography accurately later. A catalogue entry and a student's bibliographic card taken from that entry are shown below.

```
1 ──────  HM     ──Lee, Alfred McClung, 1906-──────────  (ed.)──── 2
          68     ──Principles of sociology.  Co-authors: ─────── 3
15 ──            Herbert Blumer and others  Introd. by ──── 4
          P34
14 ──     1964   Samuel Smith.  2d. ed.─rev. New York, ──── 5
                 ── Barnes & Noble 1964
8 ──────                                                       6
9 ──────         ── xxiii, 360p.  (College outline series, 26)──── 7

                 Published in 1946 under title: New outline ──── 12
10 ──            of the principles of sociology.            ──── 13
                 Includes bibliography.──

11 ──            ──1. Sociology
```

The book, titled *Principles of Sociology* (15) is edited (3) by Alfred McClung Lee (1). Lee was born in 1906 (2) and was still living when this entry was made. The text was co-authored by Herbert Blumer (4) and introduced by Samuel Smith (5). The 1964 text is a revised second edition (6). It was published in New York by Barnes and Noble (8). The preface and introduction cover 23 pages (9) and the main text 360 (10). The book is number 26 of a series of publications (7). Since it was previously published in 1946 (12) under another title, you may want to search the 1946 title if the 1964 title is not in the stacks. A bibliography is included (13) which could perhaps lead you to other books relevant to your topic. The book is catalogued only under the main LCSH of "Sociology" (11). The Library of Congress call number (14) tells you that the book is classified with sociology and indicates exactly where to find it in the library.

author's name ——

title ——

publishing details ——

call number ——

short form used in your notes

Lee, Alfred McClung   Lee

Principles of Sociology.

New York: Barnes & Noble, 1964

HM68. P34, 1964

The catalogues of other libraries are probably available at your library. Printed or microfiche catalogues of famous and well-stocked libraries such as the British Library (formerly the British Museum), the Library of Congress, and the Bibliothèque National are usually located in the reference section or the cataloguing department of academic libraries. Catalogues of local or nearby libraries may also be accessible from your library. Not all of these catalogues provide subject access to catalogued material. If they do, however, they can aid students in the preparation of working bibliographies. While the material catalogued by these other libraries may not be readily available at your own, it is worthwhile to get a broad overview of what has been published on a particular topic by consulting these catalogues. Also, it is often possible to borrow material from other libraries through your library's inter-library loan system (ILL). Keep in mind that you must place ILL orders well ahead of time in order to be sure of meeting your essay deadline. If much of the material you need to consult is only available through ILL, you should begin compiling your working bibliography early in the term.

Indexes and Abstracts

As mentioned, library catalogues do not usually contain listings of articles published in periodicals. Only the periodical's title, authoring body, and general subject heading will appear in most catalogues. Because of this convention, abstracts and indexes must be consulted. A treasure trove is unlocked when students discover that the key to finding relevant articles in journals, newspapers, and magazines is the use of indexes and abstracts.

These bibliographic tools, housed in the reference section of the library, list the articles written in specific fields in specified periodicals published over a specified period: the field is indicated in the title of the index or abstract, e.g., *Pollution Abstracts,* and the journals indexed are listed inside, probably on the first page or so. Abstracts and indexes are published periodically, with new volumes or issues appearing every month, every few months, or every year: work from the most recent issue or volume backwards in order to find up-to-date scholarship on your topic. The articles are indexed by author, which is useful if you want to know whether a particular person has published anything on the topic you are researching, and by subject heading, which is what you will use most of the time. Each listing will provide a complete bibliographic citation, which you will need in order to find the article in the library: journal name, year, volume number, issue number, and page references.

There are many kinds of indexes and abstracts. Newspaper indexes like *The New York Times Index* and the *Index to the Times* provide subject access to articles that have appeared in these two newspapers. The *Canadian Newspaper Index,* on the other hand, indexes articles that have been published by a variety of different Canadian newspapers. Some indexes will list articles that can be found in general or popular magazines, while others will index the articles in scholarly journals.

Abstracts differ from indexes in that they provide a summary or précis of the articles they list. This précis is itself called an abstract. Abstracts also tend to be more focused upon a specific discipline and more comprehensive in their coverage of the journals related to that discipline. Three entries follow: one from a newspaper index, one from an index of scholarly journals, and another from an abstract. Examine these entries and note the accompanying bibliographic cards made from them.

Extract from a newspaper index.

CANADA:—
—— Death of One of the few Titled Canadians—
Lafontaine, 31 *m* 11 *e*
—— Defence of, Notes about, 15 *a* 5 *d*—17 *a* 5 *c*
—— and Lord Monck, 14 *m* 10 *c*
—— the Ministers Banquetted on their Return
to the Dominion, 7 *j* 12 *d*
—— New Goldfields in, Fine Specimen Exhibi-
ted in Toronto, 1 *a* 10 *b*
———— Notes about, 18 *a* 10 *f*   .
—— Preparations against a Fenian Raid, 1 *a*
12 *a*
—— *Toronto Globe* on the Cessian of Russian
America, 19 *a* 9 *f*
—— Troops in, 15 *a* 5 *d*
Canadian Confederation, 23 *m* 11 *d*—23 *m* 12 *c*

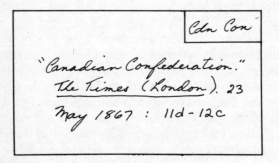

Cdn Con

"Canadian Confederation."
The Times (London). 23
May 1867 : 11d - 12c

Extract from a scholarly journal index.

Thomas, Aquinas, Saint, 1225?-1274
    See also
    Neo-scholasticism
                    about
Aquinas on infinite regresses. T. J. Day. *Int J Philos
Relig* 22 no3:151-64 '87
Aquinas on the ontological status of relations. M. G.
Henninger. *J Hist Philos* 25:491-515 O '87
The concept of worldly beatitude in the writings of
Thomas Aquinas. A. J. Celano. *J Hist Philos* 25:215-26
Ap '87
Maimonides and Aquinas on the names of God. A.
Broadie. *Relig Stud* 23:157-70 Je '87
Purity of soul and immortality. K. L. Schmitz. *Monist*
69:396-415 Jl '86
Theological exegesis and Aquinas's treatise "against the
Greeks". M. D. Jordan. *Church Hist* 56:445-56 D
'87
Thomas Aquinas's derivation of the Aristotelian categories
(predicaments). J. F. Wippel. *J Hist Philos* 25:13-34
Ja '87
The unity of adequate knowing in St. Thomas Aquinas.
J. H. Robb. *Monist* 69:446-57 Jl '86
Uses and misuses of the term "social justice" in the
Roman Catholic tradition. N. J. Paulhus. bibl *J Relig
Ethics* 15:261-82 Fall '87

Robb, J.H.   *Robb*

" The unity of adequate
knowing in St. Thomas Aquinas"
The Monist.   69 (July 1986)
: 446-457

*Humanities
Index
V. 14*

Extract from an abstract.

3114. VERSTAPPEN, HERMAN T. (Int. Inst. Aerospace Surv. Earth Sci., P.O. Box 6, 7500 AA Enschede, Neth.) J COASTAL RES 4(4): 573–587. 1988. [In Engl. with Engl., Span., Fr. and Ger. summ.] **Old and new observations on coastal changes of Jakarta Bay [Indonesia]: An example of trends in urban stress on coastal environments.**—Since the author surveyed the coastal environment of Jakarta Bay in the 1950s, rapid urbanization has affected both the alluvial plain that borders the bay and the coral reefs in it. The urban stress factors are diverse and include baywater pollution, the use of beach and coral debris for construction, the implementation of major engineering works (harbour extension, storage lake), intensified fishing and tourism and, within the Jakarta connurbation, groundwater extraction resulting in land subsidence of as much as 4–5 cm/year. Natural stress factors also have occurred and relate to an anomalous behavior of the InterTropical Convergence Zone (ITCZ), resulting in very low precipitation and relatively strong northerly and easterly winds during the 1960s and 1970s. The coastal environment was unable to absorb the combined stress factors and substantial change and deterioration thus resulted. The causative factors are weighed and an outlook for the future is given.

Verstappen, Herman T.   *Verst*

" Old and new observations on
coastal changes of Jakarta Bay:
An example of trends in urban
stress on coastal environments."
Journal of Coastal Research.
4.4 (1988) : 573-587
*Biological
abstracts
X.87 ❧3114*

Obviously, articles discovered using indexes and abstracts can aid a student's research effort greatly. By using a newspaper index, a history student would be able to find pieces published in the *Times* during the early nineteenth century concerning the abolition of slavery. A student writing an essay on employment equity for disabled persons might be able to demonstrate that media coverage of this topic has increased over the last five years by discovering how many articles on this subject were published in popular magazines during each of the years under consideration.

Students also need to use journals if they are to find the most recent scholarship in their research. Journals are the regularly published collections of articles – otherwise known as essays – by researchers currently doing work in their specific fields. The material in journals is likely to have been written less than a year before the issue is ready for circulation in the library: books, in contrast, can be five to seven years old, school age themselves, by the time they are ready for circulation. Through journal articles, many researchers and writers give their ideas their first public hearing. Journals thus represent an ongoing conversation among scientists, social scientists, historians, literary critics, and others, about current areas of experiment, debate, or discussion. Every university library has subscriptions to hundreds or even thousands of journals, each devoted to a particular area of study (perhaps an area as broad as biology or as narrow as the ecclesiastical history of Sussex), each one published periodically (usually monthly or quarterly) and at regular intervals bound into a hard-cover volume containing several issues.

Information on where these journals and other periodicals are indexed is available in *Ulrich's International Periodicals Directory*. To give you an idea of the scope of some of the larger indexes and abstracts, we have a list of them below. This list is not comprehensive. For more information, consult reference librarians or the book *Guide to Reference Books*.

Indexes

Art Index (1929-)
Arts and Humanities Citation Index (1978-)
Biological and Agricultural Index (1964-)
British Humanities Index (1962-)
Book Review Digest (1905-)
Book Review Index (1965-)
Business Periodicals Index (1958-)
The Canadian Book Review Annual (1975-)
Canadian Business Index (1975-)
Canadian Education Index (1965-)
The Canadian Essay and Literature Index (1973-)
Canadian Magazine Index (1985-)
Canadian Newspaper Index (1977-)
Canadian Periodical Index (1920-)

Computer Literature Index (1980-)
Education Index (1929-)
Energy Index (1971-)
Environment Index (1971-)
Essay and General Literature Index (1900-)
Infodex (1986-)
International Index to Film Periodicals (1972-)
International Index to Periodicals (1907-1960)
    International Index (1960-1965)
    Social Sciences and Humanities Index (1965-1974)
    Social Sciences Index (1974-)
    Humanities Index (1974-)
MLA International Bibliography of Books and Articles on the
  Modern Languages and Literatures (1922-)
The Music Index (1949-)
The New York Times Index (1851-)
Palmer's Index to the Times (London) (1790-1941)
Index to the Times (London) (1906-)
The Philosopher's Index (1967-)
Play Index (1949-)
Point de Repère (1984-)
Poole's Index to Periodical Literature (1802-1906)
Reader's Guide to Periodical Literature (1900-)
Religion Index (1949-)
Répertoire analytique d'articles de revues de Québec (1972-1984)
Science Citation Index (1961-)
Social Science Citation Index (1972-)

Abstracts

Abstracts in Anthropology (1970-)
Abstracts of English Studies (1958-)
Abstracts of Native Studies (1984-)
Aquatic Sciences and Fisheries Abstracts (1971-)
Biological Abstracts (1926-)
Chemical Abstracts (1907-)
Ecology Abstracts (1980-)
Energy Abstracts (1971-)
Economic Abstracts (1953-)
Environment Abstracts (1971-)
Geographical Abstracts (1966-)

Historical Abstracts (1955-)
Index Medicus (1899-)
International Development Abstracts (1984-)
International Political Science Abstracts (1951-)
Language and Language Behavior Abstracts (1967-)
Pollution Abstracts (1970-)
Psychological Abstracts (1927-)
Sociological Abstracts (1952-)

Once you have used the appropriate index or abstract and selected a number of articles, you will need to find out whether your library has the journals in which these articles appear. To determine this, look in the library's periodicals or serials catalogue. (Ask at the reference desk if you do not know where to find it.)

Other Bibliographies
There are many other bibliographies besides catalogues, abstracts, and indexes that could prove useful to you. Often, bibliographies or lists of works consulted appear at the end of books, articles, and reports. Close attention to the bibliographies and footnotes contained in your recommended readings can help you develop your own working bibliographies. Also, many times libraries, librarians, or researchers will compile bibliographies on specific subjects or individuals. These bibliographies are frequently published in book form and distributed to libraries where they are catalogued and shelved in the reference section. There may be "subject bibliographies" on native education, waste management, European imperialism, or Polynesian art in your library. Bibliographies of the works of well-known authors like Shakespeare, Melville, Marx, and Rousseau have certainly been compiled. Often these "personal bibliographies" contain not only lists of the writings of these famous individuals, but lists of the books and articles written about these writings and about their renowned authors.

Finding a bibliography on your particular topic can save you time. Often the compiler will have searched through the appropriate abstracts, indexes, and bibliographies before completing his or her list. If this is so, duplicating this search on your own is unnecessary. However, make sure you evaluate the comprehensiveness of the compiler's search before you decide what research you still must do. Ask yourself what kinds of information have been included in the bibliography. Does it list books, articles, dissertations, government documents, manuscripts, films, or maps? When was the bibliography published? Is the material cited recent enough to be useful? It is wise to estimate the bibliographer's cut-off dates. If the bibliography cites articles published between 1950 and 1980, for example, it may be possible for you to ignore the indexes that list articles published between these two dates. Remember too that bibliographers can be biased. One may have dismissed arbitrarily the extremely perceptive works of a scholar simply because her last name begins with "J."

Bibliographers may also evaluate the information they list. Their evaluations, called annotations, might help you to decide what material must be consulted closely and what can be skimmed. They might also assist you in determining the order in which information should be studied. Scholars often write annotated bibliographies in conjunction with their scholarship and such a bibliography would be invaluable in making research decisions.

Bibliographies can be found by consulting the "Subject" section of the library's catalogue. The subject heading of a bibliography will consist of the general subject of the bibliography followed by a "format subdivision" indicating that the catalogued item is, in fact, a bibliography. For example, a bibliography on women in Canada might be found under the subject heading "Women - Canada - Bibliography." Watch for the format subdivision "- Bibliography" when you are looking through the catalogue under subject headings relevant to your topic.

Computer Databases

Computer databases are recent research aids. Your library may have developed its own database which lists its holdings. These databases, more commonly referred to as online catalogues, have already been discussed. Even if an online catalogue is not yet available at your library, the librarians who work there probably have access to thousands of commercial and government databases. These databases can be divided into four types: full text databases (which store the complete texts of newspaper articles, speeches, encyclopaedias, and dictionaries); numeric databases (which store government and financial statistics, stock market figures, and other numeric data); directory databases (which provide information about companies, associations, individuals, and sometimes even chemicals); and bibliographic databases (which store citations of print and non-print information sources).

Searching a bibliographic database can help a student prepare her or his working bibliography. However, since many bibliographic databases correspond to printed indexes and abstracts, a student must decide which form of bibliography would yield the best results. A computer search is generally advisable if you must consult the most recently published information. Also, because many databases allow searchers to look for words in the complete record, a newly developed or rare term that might not have been included in a printed abstract's index could be located during a computer search. For example, a student searching through the printed version of *Psychological Abstracts* for articles on backward chaining might have to scan through the thousands of citations listed in this abstract's index under "behaviour modification" looking for the words "chaining" or "backward chaining." A computer could perform this task with more accuracy and speed. Computer searches have disadvantages as well. They often cost money, and you therefore cannot afford to browse through records. In addition, because computer databases are relatively new, they will probably not list citations of information published before a certain date. If you are looking for articles written during World War II, for example, a traditional search using printed indexes and bibliographies would be more effective than a computer search.

Generally, you will not be able to perform your own computer search. Since there are so many different databases to choose from, and since each database has its own peculiarities and often its own command language, librarians usually search computer databases for students. This is particularly the case if the database to be searched is remote from the library and must be accessed through a commercial database supplier over telephone lines. Such searches must be well-planned and quickly executed since the searcher is generally charged by the amount of time he or she is connected to the database and by the amount of information retrieved.

To avoid passing on these charges to students, libraries will occasionally purchase complete databases or portions of databases and store them on a local computer. New technology which allows masses of information to be stored in a relatively small space has made this option more realistic. The database may come to the library on tape or on CD-ROM (Compact Disk-Read Only Memory), and it may be updated regularly. Ask your reference librarian about computer databases that your library or institution owns.

Regardless of the kind of database you would like to have searched, or of who owns the database and where it is stored, any computer search is performed using similar strategies. The searcher asks the computer to look through its records for words or phrases that describe specific concepts. Sets of concepts are formed and related to one another through the use of "logical operators" such as "and," "or," and "not." Imagine that you are searching *PAIS (Public Affairs Information Service)* for citations on American responses to terrorism. You would first have to think of all the ways that the concepts "American" and "terrorism" could be represented and form two sets of words and phrases by using the "or" operator.

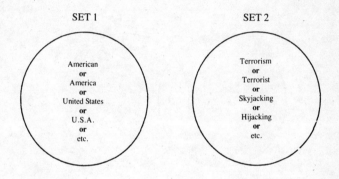

Next, you would ask the computer to look for the intersection of these two sets by using the "and" operator.

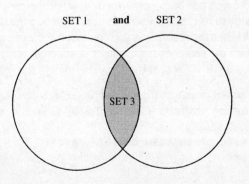

Now imagine that the results of this search are being printed. A ream of paper loaded with citations is spewing onto the library floor, offending both your sense of neatness and your ecological principles. You suddenly realize that half the citations retrieved deal with Latin American responses to terrorism. After a mad but successful scramble to press the computer terminal's interrupt key, the searcher turns to you and says, "Your search strategy must be refined." You might do this by using the "not" operator to eliminate the following concepts: South America, Central America, and Latin America.

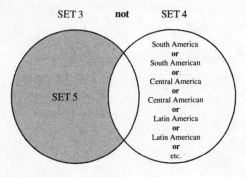

There are many other ways to make bibliographic searches more specific. They can be limited by the date the material cited was published, by its language, and by its type. Students can request that only review articles, government documents, and dissertations be found, for example. Librarians will guide you through the intricacies of developing an appropriate search strategy and choosing which databases to search.

Once the search has been performed, you will be provided with a printed version of its results. These results might be printed at the time of the search when the searcher is still "online," or they may be printed "offline" when the searcher is no longer connected to the computer. Offline prints are usually sent by first class mail to the searcher.

Below is a section from an offline print of a search done on DIALOG file 39: Historical Abstracts (Copyright ABC-Clio).

```
827439    23A-01374
A GERMAN VIEW OF ENGLISH SOCIETY: 1851.
Arnstein, Walter L  Arnstein, Walter L.
Victorian Studies 1972 16(2): 183-203.
```

827426   23A-01361
ROBERT WALSH IN FRANCE.
Woodall, Guy R   Woodall, Guy R.
Maryland Hist. Mag. 1976 71(1): 86-92.

827351   23A-01286
THE BRITISH IN PARIS.
Richardson, Joanna   Richardson, Joanna.
Hist. Today (Great Britain) 1974 25(1): 55-60.

Selecting Library Material

Once you have compiled your working bibliography, you should evaluate the material it contains. This usually means actually getting your hands on the various books, articles, and other information sources that you now know exist. In some libraries you can go to the stacks (the shelves where library material is stored); in others you must ask for the required items at the circulation desk. If you are allowed to retrieve library resources on your own, do not neglect to browse through the relevant sections of the stacks. Information found by browsing can be illuminating; it might completely redirect the thrust of your research by providing a perspective on your topic that is new to you. A few words of caution: browsing can cause meals to be missed and night to fall unnoticed.

Regardless of how you collect resources, you must survey and evaluate them. For a book, this assessment usually takes place after you have scanned the title, the table of contents, the introduction, the conclusion, the bibliography, and the index. An article should be skimmed quickly to determine its purpose or thesis, and to get an idea of the evidence it presents. You perform these tasks to decide whether the sources listed in your working bibliography are appropriate reading for your essay, and to discover how you might use them. It is also beneficial, at this point, to prepare a reading agenda that lists the books and articles you think you should read in the order in which you will read them. Following are some of the things to consider when assessing and selecting library material.

Checklist: Selecting Library Material

1. **Do not choose only general material.** Choose some books or articles that are clearly focused on your subject.

2. **Do not choose only secondary sources of information if your topic necessitates consulting primary sources.** A detailed discussion of what constitutes a primary and a secondary source can be found in the chapter on reading.

3. **Do not choose only books and articles that support one another.** If different interpretations are possible, your essay should try to take account of those that contradict your own as well as those that support it. Abstracts, tables of contents, introductions, and summaries will indicate interpretation.

4. **Choose books that are as up-to-date as the subject demands.** In some fields, such as genetics, research material dates quickly; in other fields, such as English, it does not date in the same way (instantly, slowly, or never).

5. **Do you know anything about the author's reputation for scholarship or biases?** Check the bibliography or reference list. Has the author taken major works into account? Is she or he mentioned in other people's works? In what connection? Make sure that the author is scholarly if you are planning to use this author as an academic authority. It is possible that your essay topic requires you to investigate the opinions of popular writers, scientists, psychologists, philosophers, and historians, but do not misuse their work. Scholars provide evidence to back up assertions, and citations to back up evidence; popular writers may not. For this reason, your instructor will tend to view the scholarly writer as the more authoritative.

6. **What press published the book?** Different presses have different priorities. Learn to recognize which publishing houses regularly publish scholarly books. The information in these books may be more reliable and will be better documented.

7. **What periodical does the article appear in?** Do you know anything about its biases or its reputation? *The New Internationalist* is likely to publish articles of a different perspective than the *Financial Post*, for example.

The process of evaluating a text's significance and usefulness does not end here. As you continue to scrutinize the library material you have selected as pertinent to your topic and thesis, you must constantly think critically about it. A fuller understanding awaits a closer reading.

CHAPTER FOUR
Reading

Although most secondary and post-secondary students know how to read, very few of us spend much time thinking about the act of reading. If questioned, we would probably say that we read in order to discover an author's ideas. In fact, what we learn from reading is not simply what the author intended; we also derive meaning as a result of our interaction with the text. Sometimes the author's intent and our interpretation are one and the same; often, they are markedly different.

That reading involves the interaction of text and reader has important ramifications for the essayist. It suggests, first of all, that in order to learn the most from a text, one must read it actively and critically. The passive reader accepts what the author says and therefore limits comprehension; the active reader can move beyond what the author writes to see its implications. Secondly, that meaning is created in the interaction between text and reader implies that the reader can take control of the text. He or she need not bow to the demands of the unseen author by reading a text in its entirety. In fact, the reader can decide both what to read and how to read it.

In this chapter, we focus on both efficient reading and critical reading, providing strategies which allow the researcher to use texts to maximum advantage. The advice we offer may alter your image of reading as a relaxing and effortless act, but we think you will find the reading process more rewarding as you learn to involve yourself in it.

Concentration

Any kind of reading, whether critical or efficient or both, requires that you pay attention to what you read. It is possible to go through the motions of reading and fail to comprehend a single word: the eyes go over the words, line by line, page by page; half an hour elapses before you read, "The butler did it." "Did what?" you ask, and only then realize that your eyes may have been moving, but your mind has been astral travelling. You reread the last twenty pages and find that you have missed a murder, a religious conversion, and an avalanche.

Attending to the task of reading requires that you counteract the natural tendency of the human mind to seek the easiest route. This tendency has been responsible for many fine innovations, perhaps for our survival as a species, but it contributes little to the process of reading. Do not sit back in an armchair, book in one hand and potato chips in the other, hoping to absorb what you need to know. The mind absorbs very little indeed. In fact, the mind is excellent at screening out, dismissing as unimportant, and otherwise shirking the work of remembering and integrating new information and ideas. It has to be: the mind gets tens of thousands of pieces of information every day – sights, sounds, smells, touches, tastes – and dismisses most of them as old hat, or maybe as not appreciably different from old hat. Without this automatic selection process which separates the familiar from the unfamiliar, we would live in an hallucinatory, chaotic state, beset by a constant onslaught of images flooding in through the associative process whenever we think or notice anything. It is good, ultimately, that we screen, but the tendency means that we must work hard to absorb anything in a useful way.

You can force your mind to work harder by taking the following approach when you read. First, review the title and table of contents of the work at hand to get an overview of the material. Then, instead of reading for hours at a time, read for shorter sessions. The length of these should be determined by your purpose. If you want to recall details from your reading, half hour sessions are best; if you need overall argument, longer sessions may be more appropriate. Stop for five minutes after each session to take notes, to think about what you've read, to try to recall the main points. (The mind's capacity to accommodate new information before it must do something to hold onto it is limited.)

Once you have finished a text, review all of your notes. Try to recover a sense of the overall structure of what you have read. The mind is much better at remembering something new when: a) it has done something with it, and b) it can place pieces into a structured whole.

Part One: Efficient Reading

Reading actively to promote concentration is important, but the effective essay writer must also develop some skills for reading efficiently. For many students, completing the research for a paper is the most enjoyable part of the essay-writing process. Essays, however, have deadlines, so the temptation to indulge in reading's sensual pleasures must be resisted, at least to some extent. The amount of reading and research you do is determined by the time restrictions placed on you. Consequently, learning to read efficiently is often as necessary a skill as learning to write effectively.

The phrase "efficient reading" might conjure up images of timers and multiple-choice comprehension quizzes, but it should not be confused with speed-reading. To read efficiently is to adjust how you read to what you read. Before you open the book or begin the article, you should be able to say what you need to know from it. It is not always necessary to consider every word; sometimes ten minutes of skimming is sufficient to extract what is relevant in a text. The key to efficient reading is thus flexibility in reading rate: adapt your speed to a consciously-defined purpose. Naturally, the more detail you require from your text, the slower your reading pace may be. You should be aware, however, that slower is not always better; skimming and scanning techniques will also be appropriate for certain kinds of material and reading purposes.

Organization and Agenda

For both primary and secondary reading, the first step in reading efficiently involves the selection and organization of reading material.[1] Not all works need a thorough reading; by determining and maintaining

---

[1] The distinction between primary reading and secondary reading depends on context. In its broadest sense, primary reading is the material which you will consider in your essay; secondary reading is anything that comments upon the topic or thesis statement which you have devised from your primary sources. For example, the primary materials for an essay on Sir Walter Scott's poetry are his poems; biographies of Scott and literary criticism of his work would be secondary material. An essay which compares the various biographies of Scott, however, would rely on those biographies as the primary source and may make reference to the literary works almost secondarily. Likewise, the primary material for a descriptive essay on acid rain would come from government documents and scientific reports; secondary material would include journal articles and texts which interpret the facts found in these documents. But if a writer wished to discuss differing perceptions of the problem of acid rain in Canada and the United States, the primary sources would come from magazine and newspaper articles. Sometimes you will be asked to focus entirely upon primary sources in your essay. In that case, the analysis of those sources will come from you, rather than from other experts.

a clear purpose while you read, you should be able to avoid collecting that wheelbarrow full of notes which only clutters your desk and mind.

As you worked your way through library catalogues, abstracts, and government documents preparing a tentative bibliography, you obtained a formidable list of materials, all of which appear to be valuable and relevant. The temptation is to open the work with the shiniest cover and begin reading. But if you are to maintain control of the reading process, you must have more discipline.

Begin the task of reading by surveying each piece of material you have deemed worthy of retrieval. Look at the title, the table of contents, the introduction, the conclusion. Try to arrive at an understanding of the thesis in each article or book. Then, arrange the texts and other sources in the order in which you intend to consult them, using your thesis as a guide to determine priorities. You have now compiled a reading agenda, a guide which should prevent you from devoting too much time to material only indirectly relevant to your proposed paper.

The rate at which you read the texts selected will vary along a spectrum, depending on the importance of the material perused. At this point, you should determine reading rate for each text. The data from which you derive your own argument, for example, needs to be thoroughly understood, so it demands strategies for *detailed understanding*. After all, you want your ideas to be as water-tight as possible. Chances are, however, that the works that comment upon the initial data will begin by reviewing material with which you are already familiar. For these articles or books you can use your skimming skills to deal with information related to your own ideas but not forming their foundation, information of which you need *general knowledge*.

Once you have separated documents which require detailed study from those which may be skimmed, draw up a schedule which not only lists the readings in order of importance but also includes the amount of time you think necessary for each reading. Be flexible and realistic; don't force yourself to snap the book shut if you exceed the allotted time by ten minutes or even a half hour. The key is to avoid the reading trap — take control of the material before it devours you.

Reading for Detailed Understanding

To acquire a thorough understanding of a text, be aware of your reading process as you go through the work. It is not enough to slow down, for in reading slowly you may lose the thread of the author's argument. Rather, try to read actively. You should not allow the words simply to wash over you; neither should you memorize them. Instead, ask questions of the text and try to incorporate the responses into your existing knowledge. Force yourself to think about material from a critical perspective and to interact with it.

Active reading can be facilitated by considering the way an author has constructed the text. Writers have similar goals: all want to present arguments or relay data comprehensibly and persuasively. Hence, an author uses many of the same techniques for written expression that we discuss in this book: thesis, underlying structure, appropriate arrangement of ideas, logical paragraph development. As with other aspects of the essay-writing process, it is greatly to your advantage when reading to understand how everything fits together before focusing on one particular paragraph, then another, and so on. Part of the reading process is architectural: if you try to imagine the structure of the text you are about to read, you will be better able to understand how the pieces fit together while you are reading. This practice improves both memory (the mind's capacity for recollecting unrelated items is gnat-like) and comprehension, to say nothing of reading pleasure. Just as the writer keeps the reader in mind, the reader keeps the writer in mind. Your initial questions should be "Who is writing?" and "For what purpose?"

The points of advice that follow will allow you to detect organizational structure and are useful in a close reading of central material. They will lead to as much comprehension as the writer's degree of clarity allows. Because you should look at the whole to understand its parts, the three steps outlined below move from the general to the specific. For detailed understanding, it is probably appropriate to follow the entire sequence.

1. *Survey the work.* Remember, the author wants you to be able to understand the argument made, and will have tried to make that argument apparent. A quick glance through the work should permit you to predict the nature of the ideas presented. Here's what to look at:
   a) *The title.* A title such as "Spruce Bud Worm: Much Ado About Nothing" suggests not only the topic, but also the direction of the thesis. The author evidently believes that the aforementioned beast is not a serious threat – a useful piece of information which will help you to forecast the nature of the evidence in the paper.
   b) *Table of contents/subject headings.* A good table of contents is like an outline: it will indicate the shape of the author's argument. What is considered first? Last? Which sections are the largest?

What gets short shrift? Knowing this sort of information before you begin reading will make you more alert to an author's biases.

c) *Introduction.* An author's introduction is just like yours. It should contain a thesis, or establish the terrain to be explored, and state priorities. Sometimes the author will explain how the present work fits into existing scholarship in the field: for instance, the author may distinguish his or her argument from that of other scholars, or identify to which scholars the piece is indebted for specific ideas. The introduction is often used to justify the book's existence and to explain to the reader how and by whom the book should be read. If it is written well, the introduction will act as a guide for the entire text, rather like an instructor's introductory lecture on a subject.

d) *Conclusion.* Again, if it is written properly, the conclusion should provide a good sense of the author's argument, where it ends up, and what the author considers most important about the subject.

Surveying the text is essential preparation for the more detailed reading which follows. You now have a context – a place prepared – for the information you will acquire in a more detailed reading.

2. **Determine your purpose.** Reading for research is not reading for pleasure, although it can be pleasurable. You have a specific purpose in reading a text; before you begin to read, determine what that purpose is. For example, if you are writing on an assigned essay topic, review the questions asked by the professor. Compile your own set of questions as well. Knowing what you want to discover will allow you to read more actively, to pay particular attention to the passages most relevant to your purpose, and to skip what is irrelevant. The reader who does not have a purpose in mind quickly sinks into the text, losing stride, or skims it frenetically, gaining nothing of use.

3. **Read for meaning.** As we have said, writing effectively on any topic demands a sound understanding of the material. Dense prose, however, can sometimes seem incomprehensible; lengthy sentences, unfamiliar words, and archaic diction frequently obscure meaning. Use your knowledge of essay structure and language to decipher difficult passages.

a) *Check for patterns of rhetorical and organizational development.* Is the author dealing with a subject chronologically? Is there a movement from general to specific ideas? Is there a cause and effect development? Pay particular attention to transitional words and phrases, for they can supply a context for the sentence or paragraph to come. You can find more information about methods of development and transitions in the chapters on prewriting and drafting.

b) *Use paragraph structure to decipher a passage.* Every author knows that a paragraph should contain one main idea. Try to determine what that idea is. If you are lucky, the author will have provided a topic or summary sentence to do this work for you.

c) *Deconstruct the sentences* if the prose is particularly difficult, or if the sentences are extremely complex. Read aloud through difficult passages, concentrate on key phrases, try to parse the sentence. Often, knowing the subject and verb of a thirty-word sentence can unlock its meaning.

d) *Keep a dictionary close at hand* as a matter of course — and use it! In some disciplines, a glossary of terms may be helpful. Look up any words essential to your comprehension and write the relevant definition in a notebook devoted to the purpose. In fact, whenever you read, jot down any words you decide to look up later. Set aside half an hour a week to find and transcribe definitions for them.

Detailed understanding should be your first aim in reading central material, and gaining such comprehension may occupy a good deal of your research time, no matter how effective your reading methods. Do not be dismayed. Keep in mind that you must comprehend as thoroughly as possible the material that forms the basis of your argument. It is to your advantage that your ideas be well-founded.

Reading for General Knowledge

Not all material, however, is central. A strategy such as skimming can help you to work quickly through more peripheral material, and most readers skim without realizing it. Skimming is what we do when we flip through *The National Enquirer* in the grocery store looking for the juiciest bits. However, academic journals and books are not usually constructed with inflammatory headlines and tell-tale subheadings, so, once you have separated central from supplementary texts, you need to know how to cope with the latter.

A skilled reader skims for two reasons: either to locate a specific piece of information or to grasp the main ideas and a few significant details in a selection. Before you decide to skim, then, determine your purpose, just as you would before you read for detailed understanding. In skimming, however, your purpose should be quite narrow.

If you consult a dictionary for a word, or an encyclopaedia or other reference work to find the date of an event, for example, you will skim. Your eye skips down the page until it meets with the relevant word or numbers. Whenever you use this technique, be sure you keep in mind the precise detail for which you are searching. The active mind will naturally want to continue from Napoleon to narcissism. Don't get sidetracked!

More frequently, however, your purpose in essay research calls for skimming which will enable you to get the gist of an argument without noting all its supporting details. You will probably use this technique if your reading agenda indicates that an article might be useful but need not be read thoroughly, or if a book chapter contains nothing new but may be too important to your essay to risk eliminating from your agenda. This could be the case with an article or a book that your instructor has mentioned or one to which your other readings make reference. Skimming for main ideas and important details involves techniques quite different from skimming for a specific fact. Most readers skim through articles or chapters using the following steps: [2]

1. *Skim* the introductory paragraph(s) to establish the author's thesis or locate the thesis statement.

2. *Read* the first sentence or two of each paragraph to give you the main idea of the paragraph. Together, these should show the pattern of thesis development.

3. Let your eyes *scan* the paragraphs noting names, dates, and numbers to fill in one or two details.

4. *Read* the concluding sentence of each paragraph, especially if you do not yet have a fairly clear idea of the paragraph.

5. To remember what you have skimmed, make a brief three or four sentence *note* describing the essence of the article and considering how it might be relevant to your essay.

---

[2]Books may also be skimmed using this method, but exert some caution. You will need to read the introductory and concluding chapters in their entirety to feel confident in your knowledge of the argument made.

Whether you skim or read for detailed understanding, be sure that you keep your purpose in mind. If you use your thesis to monitor what and how you read, you should be able to make the best use of limited time. Leave passive pleasure reading for post-essay exhaustion or warm summer afternoons at the lake.

Exercise One: Reading for Detailed Understanding

We have described a three-step approach to reading for detailed knowledge: survey the text, determine your purpose, and read for meaning. To test the validity of this method, try the following experiment. Read one chapter of a textbook through from start to finish, without using this method. After you have finished, jot down what you remember of the chapter. Then read another chapter, this time using the three-step approach. Again, jot down what you recall from your reading. Compare the results.

Exercise Two: Reading for General Knowledge

A good deal of information can be gleaned from a text using the surveying method described above: looking at the title, the table of contents, the introduction, and conclusion. To test this out, pull an unfamiliar book from a library shelf. Survey it for fifteen minutes, and then record what you have discovered. What is the central thesis of the text? Is the work a scholarly or popular publication? How could the text be used in an essay?

Part Two: Critical Reading

No matter what the nature of your reading material, whether directly related or tangential, you should not accept it as absolute truth. There is room for disagreement in every academic subject: scientists argue with each other through the vehicle of equally factual articles, and certainly much writing done in the humanities can be described as the presentation of particular points of view. As you have probably already discovered, language is a powerful tool; the most feeble argument can sound convincing if masked in eloquent prose. To read effectively, therefore, and certainly to analyze perceptively, the student must be prepared to interact with the text. Try always to assume a skeptical position the moment your eyes rest on a page of print: remind yourself that paper will not refuse ink. Evaluate whatever you read; think of the material from the point of view of its context, its author, and its argument. At the same time, be conscious of your own perspective and bias. To increase your sensitivity to an argument's merit, keep the following points in mind as you read.

Your Own Prejudices

It is too simple, when confronted with an argument contrary to one's own beliefs, to reject it out of hand. To respond thus is particularly inappropriate in essay research, because an instructor expects students to address opinions divergent from their own. The work of Karl Marx cannot be dismissed simply because you have undying faith in the capitalist system. Judge an argument on its own merits; do not allow your biases and preconceptions to interfere with your evaluation. The poet Coleridge, a voracious reader and astute critic, followed this maxim: "Until you understand a writer's ignorance, presume yourself ignorant of his understanding."[3]

The Context of the Work

Where a reading comes from and who it is written for, often affect its meaning. For this reason, it is crucial to place any work in context, to consider its origins.

For example, were you writing a paper on eugenics (the belief that only certain segments of society should be allowed to procreate), placing the work of authors who support this belief in context would be essential to treating their work fairly and accurately. Francis Galton, who is usually considered the founder of the eugenics movement, sincerely believed that eugenics was necessary for the improvement of humankind. Today, the consensus in Western society is that any sort of eugenics policy would be completely unacceptable. To understand why Francis Galton believed what he did is to understand the context in which he wrote. Modern attitudes toward eugenics are shaped largely by what we now know about environmental influences, heredity, and the political dangers of a eugenics policy, information that was not available to Francis Galton. Were you writing a paper which argued that

---

[3] Samuel Taylor Coleridge, *Biographia Literaria*, ed. George Watson (London: J.M. Dent & Sons, 1971) 134.

controlled procreation should be permitted in some circumstances (although it is hard to imagine that anyone would), using Francis Galton's ideas to defend your thesis would thus be inappropriate, since he was not privy to the same knowledge as you are.

Conversely, were you arguing against eugenics, you would also have to judge Galton within the framework of his historical context. That is, you might still say that his beliefs were morally wrong, but you would recognize that, were he alive today, he might not have held those beliefs.

Even when you are working primarily with contemporary publications, context can be important. The journal in which an article appears, for example, may affect how you interpret it. Scholars still exist who support eugenics, and their articles are published, albeit in journals whose audience may be very limited. You may use these articles, but read them critically; again, remember that the printed word is not always accurate.

The best means of recognizing context is to read widely on your topic from as many diverse sources as possible. By comparing your readings, you will soon be able to determine the context in which each of them was written.

The Author's Approach

As you know, authors usually write about ideas they believe, and their writing is invariably affected by their beliefs. Look for subtext. Try to determine not only what an author is saying, but also what preconceived notions allow the author to arrive at the stated opinions. In particular, focus on the following:

1. *Intent*
   What does the author hope to accomplish? To convince the reader of something? To arouse sympathy? To inspire indignation? If the author is making an argument, what is it? Does it achieve its purpose? Remember, authors use language to further their intent, so if you determine direction, you can better perceive purposeful emphases on some aspects of the topic and polite ignorance of others. You can anticipate, for example, that a writer trying to protest the seal hunt will ignore the facts that chickens and cows suffer fates as grim as do seals, and that some Newfoundland residents depend on the hunt for their livelihood.

2. *Attitude*
   How seriously does the author take the material and the readers? A

writer for *A Star-Gazer's Guide to the Heavens* may presume the reader to be unquestioning; an astronomer published in the *University of Toronto Quarterly* will expect the reader to be critical.

3. *Tone*

Is it serious, lighthearted, condescending, ironic? Beware of tone, for it can be a persuasive tool. A condescending writer can make the reader feel stupid for not agreeing with the position advanced; a lighthearted writer can be convincing simply by virtue of a pleasant tone.

4. *Bias*

Does the author show any prejudice in the selection and interpretation of evidence? Watch for the issues an author avoids, and the ones dwelled upon. An article discussing major Canadian authors that mentions only anglophones is open to criticism. Bias is, however, usually more subtle; the alert critical reader will watch for it at every turn.

5. *Assumptions*

Assumptions are values or opinions that the writer has already "taken up" into his or her thinking, and on which part of the argument put forth is constructed. They are not addressed directly within the paper in question, although the author might well have thought carefully about the matter beforehand. Often the assumption is connected with a broad philosophical, political, or religious allegiance. For example, authors of some newspaper editorials in the 1960s criticized universities for not taking disciplinary action against faculty and students who participated in anti-war demonstrations. One of their assumptions — that the role of universities is to defend rather than challenge the authority of government — was based on a philosophical notion about the nature of democracy.

6. *Implications*

Are certain judgements and conclusions suggested without being stated directly? These are the ideas "implicit" to an argument: "entangled" in it but never explicitly acknowledged. When a federal official calls for environmental reform, the implication is that government money will have to be spent. Whereas arguments are built on assumptions, arguments include implications.

Strategies for Persuasion

Most writers use a range of strategies to convince their readers. Many of these strategies in themselves are not faults; on the other hand, they do not take the place of convincing evidence and sound argument. Authors convince either by being logical and objective or by *sounding* logical and objective. Make sure your sources are all that they seem. Remember, if you are not reading critically, an author may affect you more by style than by content.

1. *Use of Language*

   Denotations and Connotations. Writers choose words not only for their literal meanings but also for their acquired meanings and associations. Be careful to distinguish between the denotation and connotation of words. For example, we all know what the words "soda pop" denote. What they connote, however, is the memory of a bygone era, and thus they are often used by writers to evoke nostalgic sentiment.

   Up-labelling and down-labelling. These involve the use of particular words to create favourable or unfavourable responses. "Matchbox" is a down-label for a house of modest size; "cosy home" is an up-label.

   Innuendo and implied statement. This rhetorical strategy could be used to manipulate the reader's response. An example might be, "Of course, considering his past, X would not be as supportive of drunk-driving legislation as most of us would."

   Figurative language. This strategy can make meaning more vivid, which is fair enough as long as the image accurately reflects the situation it renders. "A tiny cherub weeping softly" figures the literal crying child rather differently than "a howling five-year old monster." Which phrasing is more figuratively appropriate depends on the actual behaviour of the child or upon the author's purpose in describing the scene.

2. *Use of Authorities*

   Do not accept authorities unquestioningly: they may be quoted or paraphrased out of context. Furthermore, since authorities do not always agree with one another, the word of one is not necessarily indisputable. Sometimes authors invoke the sound of authority with expressions such as "Research has proven that ..." or "History shows that ...." Evidence that is introduced in this way may be accurate, but you should be wary of it. The authority of personal experience (and of 2nd, 3rd, or nth hand experience) should also be questioned: is there more solid evidence that supports or disputes this material?

3. *Opinions and Generalizations*
Watch for unsubstantiated opinions and generalizations. Do not be fooled by a writer who masks a weak argument with an apparently methodical and logical approach.

4. *Appeals*
Recognize when the author is appealing to your sense of pity, indignation, or outrage, rather than to reason. A sincere author can be sincerely wrong.

Errors in Reasoning

When an essay topic demands a critical examination of an article or book (in philosophy or historiography, for example), you may wish to give an author's argument even closer scrutiny. The most astute scholar will occasionally employ faulty reasoning to arrive at conclusions, and discovering these errors can permit you to discount an entire thesis.

The ability to perceive reasoning errors is also an essential skill in consumer society. The effectiveness of many advertisements and sales pitches depends upon the failure of the client to detect an illogical argument. Learn to recognize the following errors and you will have a formidable defence against any pedlar of vacuum cleaners or encyclopaedias.

1. *Is the author avoiding the question?* Does she or he talk around the problem without coming to terms with it? You probably do this yourself. When confronted by an instructor who demands an explanation for a late paper, you may supply a list of all the great ideas you have for a thesis, without adding that the paper is late because you spent the weekend at a skateboarding tournament or a rowing regatta.

2. *Is the author begging the question?* Is the evidence the same as the conclusion; or, in order to accept the evidence, must you already accept the conclusion? An example of begging the question would be a politician saying, in reference to Arctic sovereignty, "American oil tankers have a perfect right to travel through international waters." The debate in this issue is about whether those waters are

international; the politician's assertion demands the reader to accept that they are.

3. *Is the author saying that something is true simply because there is no evidence to show that it is false?* This argument is a common, if illogical, defence for the existence of an omnipotent being; it can't be proven that God doesn't exist.

4. *Is the author failing to apply his or her reasoning and standards of judgement consistently?* Parents, for example, might condone premarital cohabitation in principle, but condemn it when practised by their own children. This error is known as special pleading.

5. *Is the author attempting to discredit an argument by bringing irrelevant, often personal, considerations against the other party?* "The people behind this project are wild-eyed environmentalists" is irrelevant to any essay which evaluates proposals to limit nuclear arms.

6. *Is the author indulging only in black and white thinking?* Does he or she think only in terms of extremes while ignoring the possibilities in between? Issues rarely divide themselves neatly into two opposing sides; any author who endeavours to make this sort of division should be suspect. Such an approach, however, is common in world politics. The US is good, the USSR is evil; or, alternatively, the USSR is good, the US is evil.

7. *Is the author substituting the converse for the proposition?* This is an eloquent way of saying that the author has switched the "if" and the "then" in a statement. For example, "If you use aspirin, then you will get fast headache relief" becomes "If you get fast headache relief, then you use aspirin." A useful advertising ploy, as you can see from the example.

8. *Is the author substituting the inverse for the proposition?* Again, this error involves an if-then statement, this time making both parts negative. The aspirin example can show the effect clearly: "If you use aspirin, then you get fast headache relief" becomes "If you don't use aspirin, then you don't get fast headache relief."

9. *Is the author drawing conclusions on the basis of similarities between things which are not very similar?* An example would be "Universal daycare, like universal happiness, is difficult to implement." Daycare is not comparable to happiness, and the difficulties of achieving the two are not necessarily comparable either.

10. *Is the author being superstitious?* In philosophical terms, superstition means concluding that, because one thing follows another, it is therefore caused by the first. An author might assert, "The general decline of the Western economy is caused by the flood of females into the work force." Although Western economies have declined since women began to be paid for their labour, there is no way of proving that this situation directly caused the decline.

11. *Is the author making* non sequiturs? This catch-all phrase for the most obvious errors in logical reasoning translates as "it does not follow." A statement such as "A lot of professors drive Ladas; universities must be full of communists" typifies the *non sequitur.*

Exercise Three: Critical Reading

Take half an hour to read the following editorials critically. Determine each author's approach. Can you detect intent, attitude, tone, bias, assumptions, implications? What strategies for persuasion does each writer use? Look for emotive language, down-labelling, improper use of authorities, unsupported generalizations, and so on. Are any of the errors in reasoning listed above apparent? Describe the political perspectives of the writers. How do they see the world? How have their perspectives shaped their selection of evidence? How might a third writer have presented the same facts?

Editorial #1
Terrorism: It's Time To Say No

Discussions of terrorism have dominated the editorial page of every major newspaper during the past year. Unfortunately, the quality of these discussions has not matched their quantity. Spurred on by a desire to be perceived as "progressive thinkers," many journalists have taken an approach that is worse than ineffectual. Indeed, their discussions often condone, and may even encourage, terrorist acts.

The discussions which are most destructive emphasize the causes of terrorism. They see the problem as a political one created by an imbalance of power on the world map, by the Western powers' exploitation of their weaker neighbours. Only long-term solutions, they claim, will work. End injustice and terrorists will disappear from sheer lack of motivation.

It is naive to suppose that the injustices created by international power imbalances are any worse now than they have ever been. History has never known a time when power was evenly distributed. (And social justice for all is hardly a claim most terrorist countries could make.) Yet terrorism in its current form is a relatively new phenomenon. In emphasizing global inequities, commentators run the risk of blaming the West for its own victimization.

Terrorism should not be seen as a political problem but as an inexcusable desire on the part of a few fanatics to spill the blood of fellow human beings. The victims of terrorist acts are always innocent citizens who happen to find themselves in the wrong place at the wrong time. Indeed, very often those citizens of the West who are most concerned to help others (teachers, church workers, etc.) have been the primary target.

Terrorist groups draw their members from another pool. Many people attracted to terrorist groups are deeply unstable. (When the killers on the Achille Lauro shot an elderly, crippled man and threw him into the sea, they said they wanted to prove to the world that they had no mercy. Here we caught a chilling glimpse of the terrorist psyche.) Others join the "cause" through a misguided commitment to fundamentalist religion. But surely even the most open-minded defender of religious differences would have difficulty justifying random murder as a duty to God.

There is not time to navel-gaze about subtle causes and long-term solutions. Of course, it would be nice if the Western powers could always act with moral accountability toward their weaker neighbours. But utopia is a long way off, and too many people have died already. Recent developments do seem to have shown that something can be done — if only temporarily. When the forceful approach has been taken — witness Reagan's strike in Libya — some progress seems to have been made. Such approaches are our only hope if terrorism is to end quickly.

— *Times*, 1986

Editorial #2
Terrorism and the Politics of Just Deserts

President Reagan added another chapter to his saga of the war on terrorism recently when he appeared on television to claim victory for the forces of freedom over those of tyranny. The occasion was a Senate vote which released over $100 million to the CIA-backed Contras who are attempting to overthrow the Government of Nicaragua, a country that he describes as a terrorist state. For many of us who see Nicaragua as a little country besieged by the US throughout this century, Reagan's ability to perceive it as the bedfellow of Libya can be perplexing. Perhaps it is time for an exposition of the logic that enables his perspective.

In the Reagan mathematica, there is a simple, fundamental equation: those who defend America's military-industrial interests are freedom fighters; those who don't are the enemies of freedom. Thus, America's friends include Canada, Britain, and West Germany, but also Marcos of the Philippines, Botha of South Africa, the Duvaliers of Haiti, and the Shah of Iran. Among its enemies are Qaddafi of Libya and the people of Nicaragua.

In a further permutation of the Reagan algebra, we discover that violence committed by the US is justified; violence against it is terrorism. When Reagan called Qaddafi the mad dog of the Middle East in the wake of the Achille Lauro affair, he sensibly neglected to mention that American warships had not long before fired Porsche-sized missiles into unarmed Druze villages along the Libyan coast.

The Neoconservatives who endorse Reagan's foreign policy might argue that America would only impoverish and endanger itself in the attempt to right its international wrongs, that the Soviet bear is hungrily watching, ready to pounce at the least sign of weakness in the American chains of power. Yet the bear seems to have learned from history where the eagle has not. It has indeed made friends in Africa and in Central America, not by pouncing on the weak, Rambo style, but by feeding them. America, meanwhile, remains loyal through the eleventh hour to its infamous friends and helps them to prop up their regimes.

It is difficult to measure the exact degree of US responsibility for the violence suffered by American civilians. And someone who has not been brutalized cannot understand the rage of one who has, whether the battered woman who finally murders her husband, or the battered Libyan people who finally murder an American citizen, or the ever-gentle Bishop Tutu, who is at last moved to say, "The West can go to Hell." But when the abuse of power is clear, as it is with American foreign aggression, the exact degree is unimportant. By any calculation America is guilty enough, and continues to invite the rage it has provoked.

If America is truly determined to wage war on terrorism, it must break with the historical Western tradition of foreign aggression and military imperialism. It is high time that the Western powers learned to wage peace — not a "quick fix" perhaps, but the only one that will work. Until we do that, we can only accept terrorist attacks as our inevitable and just deserts.

— *The Monitor*, 1986

CHAPTER FIVE
Notetaking

As you read, write. A simple maxim, but one that can be profitable when applied to the task of essay research. Recording ideas and bibliographic information is, quite simply, efficient. Hours of precious day-before-due-date time can be wasted relocating that perfect quotation which captured the essence of your paper, or making one more trip to the library to obtain publication dates.

Notetaking has other advantages as well. Through writing about a text, the reader becomes more engaged than when reading passively. The act of taking notes facilitates critical reading; it demands that you understand and evaluate, continually seeking content and argument relevant to a particular focus. Notetaking can also permit the student some distance from sources, making it a useful strategy in avoiding unintentional plagiarism. The student who takes thorough notes may not even need to consult texts during the writing of the essay, the required material having already been diligently recorded.

With all these advantages to recommend it, one would think that the craft of notetaking would be perfected early in a student's career, yet the tendency is to be sloppy at this stage of the writing process. Beginning to research by copying down bibliographic information seems tedious, and pausing to paraphrase just at the moment when meaning becomes clear is frustrating. To take notes well, therefore, necessitates the acquisition of a method so meticulous, so ritualized, that the act of jotting information down becomes second nature.

General Principles

The research process involves continual oscillation between thesis and discovery. As reading and research progress, you will revise and modify your tentative thesis. Simultaneously, however, your thesis will provide direction for your reading and notetaking. Your goal should be flexibility without chaos: do investigate new paths of information, but guard against tangents that might take you completely off course. Never work without a thesis in mind. Otherwise, texts take control of you, rather than the more desirable reverse experience.

The research process reaches forward to writing as well: the shape and size of the finished essay must be considered continually so that the specific requirements of the writing task are met. As you take notes, therefore, keep an outline in mind. The aim of notetaking is not to gather a great mass of notes, but rather to gather notes directed toward a particular end. Thinking about the various areas that must be explored to establish your argument should help you to know when you have reached the point of diminishing returns. Remember, too, that your essay has a finite length, so there is no great virtue in taking many more notes than you can hope to use. At the same time, do not try to save the trees. Leave room to add comments, cross-refer to other notes, and so on.

Either index cards or ordinary paper can be used for taking notes. Many people prefer the card method, primarily because a set of note cards can be shuffled around and arranged into outline form neatly and without confusion. A second good reason for using cards is that they can be filed easily since they are all the same size and contain only one note each. Not everyone feels comfortable, however, working within the limitations of a 3 x 5 space. If you prefer the roominess of full-sized paper, use sheets of standard size so that you can keep them together.

As you write, strive for accuracy. Your final goal is to have a set of notes that you can use with complete confidence. At the same time, bring yourself to the task of notetaking; since reading is an interaction between you and the text, you should be recording not only information and opinions, but your responses to them. Your note that Jordan's theory about continental drift seems untenable will be as useful in the writing process as the quotations and summaries you have recorded.

Notetaking Method

1. *Begin by writing your tentative thesis statement or description of purpose on two 3" x 5" cards.* Post one of these cards on the wall

above your desk for the duration of the time you spend on your essay. Keep the other one in your pocket, so that it is always available for consultation. Of course, you will probably revise your thesis as you read; continue to replace the cards to reflect the revision, and keep your spirits up by anticipating the satisfaction you will feel when you can take the thesis card down.

2. *Before taking any notes on content, write the bibliographic information on its own card, one card per book, article, or other item.*[1] Usually for a book you will record author, title, publisher, place of publication, and date published. For an article, the name of the journal, the volume and issue numbers, the year published, and the page references will be necessary. You will, then, produce two varieties of cards, one for your bibliography – sometimes called "Works Cited" or "References" – and one for the text of the essay. Note the bibliographic details exactly as they will be cited in your essay; this method will enable you to put the cards in alphabetical order and to copy from them directly to produce the bibliography or works cited list. Include the library call number on your card in case you want to consult the book again. For a journal article, the source of reference might be useful. Also include a unique short form for the work – probably the author's last name and initials – and use that abbreviation when you take notes.

3. *Write down, on separate cards, the following categories of notes.* Remember to put only one point on each card. Include the short form for the source document, and the page or line reference.
   a) *Quotations.* Several restrictions apply in this category. In research papers, quotations are generally used for one of three reasons. Sometimes, the wording in a passage is so precise that it cannot be paraphrased without loss of meaning. Secondly, the person being quoted may be highly respected in the field and quoting him or her directly will help to bolster the case you are making. Conversely, you may wish to quote an authority in order to dispute an argument made. Finally, the stylistic qualities of the passage may demand comment. Consider the example of Churchill's World War II speech, "We shall fight on the beaches, we shall fight on the landing grounds, we shall fight in the fields and in

---

[1]For an example of bibliographic card format, see Chapter Three.

the streets...."[2] You might quote this passage, not to draw attention to its literal meaning, but to show that the manner in which Churchill expressed himself affected the public's response to what he was saying.

In a literature essay, quotations are used primarily to draw attention to language, although you might also quote to show an author's point of view or philosophic leanings. A literary quotation should establish the way diction or imagery or alliteration is used by the author, not how the plot is progressing.

Your own reading experience tells you that quotations must be succinct; reading nine or ten lines of single-spaced prose is difficult and irritating. Usually, if you can't write the passage on a 3 x 5 card, it is too long to quote in its entirety in the essay.

Always place quotation marks around direct quotations in your notes. Failing to do so may lead to committing unintentional plagiarism. When you are transcribing directly, two notation conventions will be useful. The first is the square bracket: [ ]. It is used to indicate that you have added something to a quotation or changed it ever so slightly in order to make its meaning more clear. For example, if your quotation read, "Cosmetic companies use this substance in foundation cream," you might write "this substance [whale blubber]" so that your reader would understand the reference. The second device, ellipsis dots (. . .), permits you to indicate that you have omitted a portion of a quoted passage.

When you take notes, guard against quoting an author out of context. Introducing ellipsis dots or quoting only a sentence fragment may allow you to distort the meaning of the passage quoted. Be true to the author's intent; any other approach is dishonest.

b) *Facts and Figures.* Be meticulous here. Check the data you are recording carefully before you return your source to the library, so that 10,000 pounds of raw sewage doesn't miraculously become 100,000 pounds in your essay. Facts and figures, incidentally, do not need to be placed within quotation marks. The reader will understand that you have borrowed the data directly, provided that you document the source.

c) *Summaries/Paraphrases.* Probably most of your notes will be of

---

[2] Winston Churchill, *Blood, Sweat, and Tears* (New York: G.P. Putnam's Sons, 1941) 297.

the summary or paraphrase variety. Many novice researchers assume that if paraphrasing means putting a passage "in your own words," this can be accomplished simply by substituting synonyms for key terms. The process is actually much more complex. Proper paraphrasing depends on thorough comprehension of material, not on a thesaurus. You must read the passage you wish to paraphrase, think about it until you understand it, and then write notes as if you were explaining the idea or issue to yourself. If you have thought about the passage carefully enough, there should be no need to consult the text again while you write the summary. For example, consider the following passage:

> Studies of twins reared apart, and of foster-children whose real parents were known, have tended to confirm that environmental conditions can have a measurable effect upon the performance of children in intelligence tests. At the same time, such studies have demonstrated that the extent of any improvement which may result from a better environment is limited.[3]

A proper paraphrase would approximate what follows: "Gregory's study of separated twins and foster-children establishes that a child's environment can affect intelligence, but probably only in a limited way." An improper paraphrase might read: "Studies of separated twins and of foster-children whose real parents are known have shown that environmental conditions can affect a child's I.Q. However, these studies have shown that the extent of any improvement caused by a better environment is marginal."

The first note shows the student's thought at work; the passage has been considered carefully and its principal idea deduced. The second note depends far too heavily on the original structure of the passage. The same information is contained in both notes, but the latter still bears the stamp and uses the words of the original source.

As you paraphrase, strive also for accuracy. Do not confuse what you want research to show with what it does show, and do not paraphrase a point out of context. In the above passage, it would be easy to ignore the second sentence and paraphrase only

[3] Robin E. Gregory, *A Shorter Textbook of Human Development* (London: McGraw-Hill, 1969) 57.

the first: environment affects intelligence. Gregory, however, makes only a qualified claim. The note must reflect the author's intent.

Make sure also that you paraphrase in a manner which will permit you to attribute information properly when you write. Attribution is the proper acknowledgement of sources and actions within the main body of an essay. Your reader will want to know both where an idea or opinion came from (who wrote about it) and who the source of an action was (who did it). For example, when an essay declares that "Ontario Supreme Court Justice, Jane Doe, reached the decision in the 1990 court case . . . ," the reader knows the person, the person's title, and the date of the decision, and is able to assess the reliability of the decision made. If, instead, the student had written, "The decision was reached in a court case," the reader would have no way to evaluate the ruling. Likewise, in the proper paraphrase above, the reader knows that the study was completed by Robin Gregory and can evaluate the results in view of that fact. The improper paraphrase does not give the reader the same privilege. Failure to attribute is not plagiarism, but it is a serious weakness in scholarship.

d) *Comments.* As we have stressed, an essay involves interaction between you and the topic. Through reading, you will gain personal insights, and will gradually develop your own opinions and perceptions. Record these insights as you read; your notes will then provide that necessary balance between yourself and the material. If you find a particular interpretation of an historical event to be the most creative and ingenious discussion you have ever read, write yourself a note explaining why. If a sociological theory helps you to understand a personal experience, write that down as well. Remember, you are reading critically, and to do that, you must interact with the material.

e) *Words that need clarification.* Make sure you understand the terms of the discussion entered into. If subsequent reading does not define them clearly, consult a specialized dictionary.

Sample Note Card:

short form keyed to bibliography card

page number

outline or index heading —— # Happiness   Rooke, 53

summary ——

quotation ——

argues that epistemological considerations are "ultimately irrelevant."

comment —— [But compare R's stance in Ch VIII, Lassie, Come Home]

Sample Note Paper:

short form keyed to bibliography

page number

summary & quotation

comments

Rooke, 53	argues that epistemological considerations are "ultimately irrelevant."	[but compare R's stance in Ch VIII, Lassie Come Home]
Rooke, 68	genius ≠ geniality	[an important distinction but not a difficult one]
Rooke, 119	ineffectuality of the intellect in a world of instant-off controls.	[use this in Section III? re "cultivate yr. own garden" tendency]

Exercise One: Notetaking

Read the following passage and consider the notes on the text which follow it. Which will be useful when the student begins to write? Which may cause problems or extra work?

> Clifford Sifton's tenure as superintendent general of Indian affairs did not occasion dramatic changes in Canadian Indian policy. He had almost no creative new ideas to offer, and most of his policy statements and administrative reforms appear to have been generated substantially within the department. It is arguable that his administrative reforms made the service more efficient, more highly centralized, and that he made a fairly steady effort to minimize the number of incompetent individuals. He left his stamp on the department in many of the leading personnel and indeed in the drastic upheaval at all levels of the staff. The changes tended to bring to power men who were if anything less sympathetic to the Indians and to place expenditure under the control of a cost-conscious bureaucracy.[4]

1. Bibliographic Card

Hall, David. "Clifford Sifton and Canadian Indian Administration 1896-1905."
in *As Long as the Sun Shines and the Water Flows: A Reader in Canadian Native Studies*
(Vancouver: UBC Press, 1983)

2. Note Card

Hall, 137
Hall says that Sifton had almost no new creative ideas to offer and that most of his work was generated substantially within the department.

3. Note Card

Hall, 137
Hall is critical of Sifton, claiming that Sifton was not innovative in the

---

[4] David J. Hall, "Clifford Sifton and Canadian Indian Administration 1896-1905," *As Long as the Sun Shines and the Water Flows: A Reader in Canadian Native Studies*, eds. Ian Getty and Antoine Lussier (Vancouver: U of British Columbia P, 1983) 136-37.

work he did in Indian Affairs and that his administrative reforms brought in personnel who were probably not that sympathetic to natives.

4. Note Card

Hall
Hall writes, "Clifford Sifton's tenure ... did not occasion dramatic changes in Canadian Indian policy."

5. Note Card

Hall, 137
During Sifton's period in office, there were few changes in Indian policy. Sifton was a good manager, and made staff changes, but the staff he recruited were bureaucrats who were unsympathetic to the natives.

Exercise Two: Paraphrasing

Consider the following passage:

> The expansion of Canadian aid programmes beyond Asia in the late 1950s was undertaken to support Britain's decolonization programme in the Caribbean and Africa. Dismantling the empire in both regions was a worrisome process and Britain was reluctant to leave its old territories undefended against possible socialist influences from within or without. Canada was asked to help out and readily agreed.[5]

Which of the following notes illustrate proper paraphrasing technique?

1. Britain invited Canada to help with aid in the Caribbean and Africa, and Canada acted without hesitation.

2. Canada's international aid increased around the period of 1955-60 because, although Britain wanted to pull out of Africa and the Caribbean, it didn't want to leave these areas entirely without support.

3. Canadian aid programmes were expanded after World War II.

---

[5] Richard Swift and Robert Clarke, eds., *Ties that Bind: Canada and the Third World* (Toronto: Between the Lines P, 1982) 154.

4. Canadian aid programmes were expanded to support England's decolonization programme in the Caribbean and in Africa.

5. Because Britain was afraid of possible socialist influences in the Caribbean and Africa upon decolonization, it sought help from Canada in the form of increased Canadian aid to these regions.

Documentation

An academic essay, at its best, forms part of a dialogue with other scholars in a discipline: ideas are exchanged, points are disputed, facts are shared and interpreted. At the undergraduate level, the essay enters the academic community not as a voice crying in the wilderness, but as one trying to make meaning out of contradictory data and dissenting opinions. The essay rarely needs to present entirely new information or ideas; rather, it brings a new mind to material already available. More concretely, no matter what your essay topic, you are not necessarily expected to uncover previously unknown information about it, but instead to contemplate knowledge already available and write about it in a manner that gives it new meaning. In Sample Essay B on lobby groups, for example, the student is not giving the instructor any factual information that could not be found in a university-level textbook on governmental systems. Rather, she is using information to make a point that the reader might not be aware of: the nature of the two systems makes the experience of lobby groups in the two countries different.

Because essays do synthesize knowledge and viewpoints of others, documentation – acknowledging the source of information obtained – performs an important function in essay writing. The need to avoid plagiarism is only one of several reasons for documenting the sources of your evidence and ideas. The others are the desire to establish the reliability of the evidence you present and to provide the interested reader with the references needed to read more on the subject. Keep in mind that your essay is a dialogue between yourself and other scholars, and it should be relatively easy to determine acknowledgements.

An analogy may help you to see the correct procedure for documentation more clearly. Imagine that you play softball, and that you are having a discussion with some of the other team members about strategies for an upcoming tournament. Everyone in the discussion will know certain facts: who plays what position, the rules of the game, the schedule of the tournament. Likewise, when you are writing an essay in a particular discipline, certain pieces of information are shared knowledge. These do not need to be documented for the same reason that you would not spend time explaining to your baseball buddies the concept of "Three strikes, you're out."

However, in your softball meeting, some facts and ideas will be known only by one person. The catcher may have developed a rationale for trying to lose the first game; if this strategy fails, you may want to remember whose idea it was. Or, the pitcher may have played in the park before and remembers that hitting a home run there is next to impossible. These ideas are put forth by single voices: they are not shared knowledge and therefore need to be attributed to particular sources.

Documentation in essays works in the same manner. Most geographers, for example, know that water temperature differs among the five Great Lakes, but only a few might be familiar with the causes for these differences. If such a fact were included in an essay, other geographers would want to know who determined these causes, again, to judge the reliability of the information provided and to inspect the research for themselves. Furthermore, particular sources must be given credit for concepts and opinions. The catcher's strategy was her idea: she'll be a little disgruntled if the right fielder claims it as his brainwave after the tournament has been won.

Once you major in a subject, or move up to the majors, you will soon develop a sense of what needs to be documented and what does not. When in doubt, though, provide a reference: you will never be penalized for providing too many. Indebtedness is not in itself shameful. It is presumed that teachers and writers have something to say that will be of use to students and readers.

Notes on the Preparation of Essays describes the two main systems of documentation used in various disciplines: the traditional endnoting/footnoting method with bibliography, and the more modern parenthetical citation with reference list. The basic difference is that in the former, sources are listed and keyed to numbers in the body of the essay, whereas in the latter, a short form for the source is indicated in brackets in the body of the text (where the number would be in the endnoting/footnoting system).

The parenthetical method is now accepted in most disciplines and required in many. Because the research done in different disciplines varies in objectives, the conventions of documentation vary a little as well. In the arts, scholars often recognize the beauty of the annotated footnote; the flow of the text is uninterrupted, but supplementary information is readily available to the curious reader.[6] In the sciences, where current research is constantly making earlier research results obsolete, the date of a publication figures more prominently than in the humanities, so the parenthetical method is more appropriate. The three sample essays in Appendix D illustrate the various methods, but see *Notes on the Preparation of Essays* for detailed instruction on exactly how to cite what in a particular discipline.

Plagiarism

Passing off someone else's words or thoughts as your own makes you a plagiarist. This is a Greek term (*plagiarius*) meaning "someone who steals someone else's child." That the academic world should have retained a word meaning "kidnapping" to denote the offence indicates its seriousness: in the case of plagiarism the kidnapper not only steals someone else's brainchild, but then pretends to be its proud parent. (Coleridge, in one of literature's more famous disputes about who wrote what, described an essay on poetry he had planned with Wordsworth as "half a child of my own brain."[7]) The act has a further grave consequence when the work is submitted for credit: the value of the degree granted by the university is undermined every time a plagiarist graduates and goes off into the world with the school's certification of competence in a field. Thus, plagiarism is extremely dishonourable, and can result in getting zero on a paper or in the course, or, in cases of repeated plagiarism, in debarment from the university. You would be in less disgrace if you were caught stealing the library's rare books collection.

At its worst, plagiarism involves presenting someone else's essay as your own, perhaps with minor modifications. It does not matter what the status of that other person is: using your roommate's essay or one you purchased from an essay-writing service is as serious an offence as submitting an article by a published scholar.

Most students are not overly anxious about the intentional plagiarism described above; here, the cheating is obvious. But many are plagued by the recognition that any failure to acknowledge indebtedness for the wording used or thought expressed in an essay is plagiarism, even if the omission is unintentional and applies only to one sentence. Such anxiety

---

[6] *Thinking It Through* uses the footnoting system for precisely this reason.

[7] Samuel Taylor Coleridge, "To Robert Southey," 29 July 1802, *Collected Letters of Samuel Taylor Coleridge*, ed. Leslie Griggs, vol. 2 (Oxford: Clarendon, 1956) 830.

is frequently compounded by the feeling that not one of the ideas in the essay is yours: all have occurred to someone else at some point.

Again, think of your essay as a dialogue among team members. The idea to lose the game is the catcher's, but the idea of agreeing with the catcher is yours. Instead of saying, "We should lose the first game," you would say, "I agree with the catcher, who says we should lose the first game (Catcher, 1989)." In an essay, you might agree with an author who believes that Trudeau made a mistake in introducing the War Measures Act; you would document the author's argument, but the fact that you were in accord would be your own idea.

Where most students err in terms of unintentional plagiarism is not in failing to acknowledge ideas, but in paraphrasing incorrectly. Stealing syntax is as significant an offense as stealing an idea because, as you know from your own writing experience, trying to phrase a point exactly is a difficult art. You can avoid this error by paraphrasing correctly as you take notes. Completely rethink a concept before you record your response to it; that way, you will be less likely to borrow word order and phraseology.

Academics are experts in reading and writing. When they suddenly encounter a plagiarized passage imbedded in a student's paper, the shift in voice is as obvious to them as if they were hearing it rather than reading it. Besides, the instructors to whom students submit essays are specialists: it is their job to read specifically in the field of instruction. They often recognize plagiarized material, and are quite rightly so incensed that if they cannot identify the source of the material immediately, they will search through the literature on the subject until they do.

Exercise Three: Plagiarism

The following quotations are all taken from a text entitled *Ethnicity in Canada: Theoretical Perspectives* by Alan Anderson and James Frideres (Toronto: Butterworths, 1981). Read each one and consider how it has been used in the student paper. Which examples show plagiarism?

1. Quotation:
    "Without realistic funding of multicultural education, as represented in second or third language instruction, ethnic-oriented histories and other textbooks, and cultural exchange programmes, it is not likely that decades of discrimination against these

minorities, usually assuming the form of enforced Anglo-conformity in the schools, will be offset" (316).

Student's Paper:

Without appropriate funding of multicultural schooling, such as instruction in second or third languages, textbooks that are oriented toward ethnicity, and cultural exchanges, it is unlikely that years of discrimination, usually in the form of Anglo-conformity, will be eliminated (Anderson and Frideres, 316).

2. Quotation:

"Again, certain groups in Canadian society, notably the most conservative ethno-religious groups, have stressed taboos to ensure fairly rigid social control which could keep members within the fold. For example, among the Mennonite and Amish people in the Kitchener-Waterloo region in Ontario, the most conservative (Old Order) sects will not use electricity, any mechanized farm machinery, or drive cars or trucks (instead they use horses and buggies)" (45).

Student's Paper:

Anderson and Frideres note that some ethnic groups, like the Mennonites and Amish, have taboos which help to keep members within the group. They cite examples such as the refusal to use cars and electricity as instances of such social controls (45).

3. Quotation:

"Canadian society, to a certain extent, exhibits some characteristics of a cultural pluralistic society. This type of system shows mutual toleration or peaceful coexistence of groups with different cultures" (297).

Student's Paper:

In that, for the most part, cultures within Canada are accepting of one another and abide together fairly peacefully, Canadian society can be said to be culturally pluralistic.

4. Quotation:

"Because of the strong institutional completeness that existed within the Japanese community before the actions taken by the federal and provincial governments, the results of the relocation were different than for the Germans nearly thirty years previously" (270).

Student's Paper:

Anderson and Frideres note that "the strong institutional completeness" existing among the Canadian Japanese prior to relocation
made the effects of government action different than they had been
for the Germans (270).

Checklist: Notetaking

1. **Record all bibliographic information before you begin to
   examine a source.**

2. **For all notes taken on a text, clearly indicate author, text, and
   page reference.**

3. **Place all direct quotations inside quotation marks. If you modify
   a quotation, use square brackets or ellipsis dots to indicate the
   changes you have made.**

4. **As you paraphrase, ensure that you do not borrow syntax or
   phraseology from the original text. What you cannot put in your
   own words, put inside quotation marks.**

5. **Keep your quotations short: try not to record passages too
   lengthy to be used as quotations in your essay.**

Following this system scrupulously will save you from both inadver-
tently plagiarizing and unnecessarily giving an author credit for your
own ideas.

CHAPTER SIX
Prewriting

Nearly every professional author describes at some point the daunting prospect of the blank page. Indeed, committing the first few words to paper seems often to be the most difficult stage in the composition process, both for novice and for experienced writers. The research may be complete, we may feel well-prepared, but the task of writing about our subject is still onerous, since it forces us to think even more carefully and completely about the topic at hand.

Writing necessitates deep thought because it requires the student to perform a juggling act, keeping several balls in the air at once. Audience needs to be considered, as does purpose. The writer must decide what ideas to present and in what order to present them, thinking all the while about how to spell "privilege" and whether a paraphrase might be more appropriate than a quotation. Little wonder that many of us shudder at the sight of an empty page.

Nonetheless, the writer can learn to approach the essay so that the agony caused by penning that initial word is lessened. In this chapter on prewriting, and in the two on drafting and revision which follow, we suggest strategies that should ease you into composition. Instead of beginning at word one and writing through to word two thousand, you will learn to resolve some demands before you begin to compose complete sentences, to ignore other demands until you are writing a final draft, and to use writing for discovery as well as for exposition.

Prewriting can loosely be defined as all the writing you do before attempting a formal draft of your essay. It serves several purposes. Some prewriting exercises will simply help you to understand your subject better; you will "know what you think when you see what you've said."

Others will help you to realize your purpose, and the standard prewriting task – the outline – will permit you to discover the best presentation of your ideas. Overall, prewriting saves time and energy. By lessening the number of demands you must consider when writing a draft, it allows you, at that stage of the essay, to concentrate more fully on developing your thesis.

Thinking and Writing Styles

Any advice on writing must inevitably be prefaced with a qualifier: every individual thinks and writes differently. This qualification is of particular relevance in a discussion of prewriting, since not everyone needs to follow the same organizational steps to begin formal composition. The written product is, inevitably, linear; we read from the left to the right, one word after the other. Some of us think about subjects in a linear fashion, too, organizing ideas in our brain similarly to the way they are organized on paper. Such writers may see many prewriting tasks as redundant, since they can explore and arrange mentally without committing words to paper. However, others of us tend toward more holistic thinking, easily perceiving the entire argument, but not necessarily in a linear fashion. Writers at this end of the spectrum may find even a formal outline imposes too rigid a structure and will be more comfortable with mind maps and free-writing techniques.

Our advice for all writers, then, is to read this chapter and experiment. Inevitably, some prewriting strategies will work well for you. Determine the extent to which you rely on linear thinking, and if prewriting strategies help you to approach that blank page with more gusto, use them every time you write.

Mind Maps

Drawing an informal and pictorial outline, sometimes known as a mind map, can be a way of freeing yourself from the constraints of sentences and paragraphs so that you can explore ideas more creatively.[1] To draw a mind map, begin by placing a tentative thesis in the centre of a blank page. Explore this thesis by drawing branches from it to represent ideas and concepts that, from your reading and research, you now

---

[1] For a full discussion of mind maps, see Tony Buzan, *Use Your Head*, rev. ed. (London: British Broadcasting Corporation, 1982) and *Use Both Sides of Your Brain* (New York: Dutton, 1983).

associate with the thesis. As you are drawing/composing your map, create as many branches as you can, and as many twigs as possible from the branches. The mind map can be used as an exploratory method only if you push yourself to explore; restricting your thinking to the main branches will never allow you to recognize the smaller, more subtle possibilities of your topic.

A mind map for *The Waste Land* sample essay might look something like this:

The mind map cannot show the order in which to pursue ideas, but it can suggest the direction of your thought, as well as the connections between ideas. Once you have sketched this kind of outline, it is often possible to recognize the sequential patterns of development needed to write a coherent draft. If your mind map indicates that you have explored your subject thoroughly, it may be possible to compose your essay directly from it.

The mind map can be useful to anyone who wants to break free of the constraints of syntax and phraseology. In particular, writers who cannot begin composing immediately in sentences and paragraphs, or who experience some difficulty with formulating complete thoughts when unsure of direction, will enjoy this prewriting strategy.

Free-Writing

As you know, writing is a means of thinking as well as a way of recording information. The linear structure of sentences and paragraphs forces us to explore ideas carefully, redefining, explaining, and focusing. Writing allows us to reflect on our subject, for, as Frank Smith notes, "Language permits thought to fold back on itself."[2] We write, think, then continue to write.

Because writing provides this opportunity for reflection, it is often useful to engage in some exploratory composition before attempting a draft. Free-writing is one such exploratory route. While it permits you to think, it still provides a temporary reprieve from the anxiety of trying to obey the rules and regulations of correct writing, allowing you to juggle one or two balls instead of four or five.

Free-writing, if less disciplined, is thus more purely exploratory than writing usually is. People often find that in free-writing they can see connections that they could not make when they were trying for perfect paragraphs or sitting in silent contemplation. A session of free-writing focused on the task of jotting down the major results of a research effort can help the writer to see what thesis emerges from those results. Some writers also use it as a sort of warm-up exercise to bring what they have in mind to the surface before they begin their day's work. Even if nothing of particular interest breaks the surface, it is often reassuring for someone suffering from a temporary writer's block to know that the pen will move across the page.

Begin free-writing by giving yourself a specific time period, say twenty minutes, so that you do not feel you are undertaking an ordeal, and write on the subject at hand for the whole time. It helps if you can focus on a specific aspect of your subject (not necessarily a small aspect). Write whatever comes into your mind; if "dumb, dumb, dumb, dumb, dumb" is all that occurs to you, then write that down. Do not stop to review what you have written and do not lift your pen from the paper (or your fingers from the keyboard). The idea is to keep yourself writing

---

[2] Frank Smith, *Writing and the Writer* (New York: Holt, Rinehart and Winston, 1982) 65.

so that your internal editor does not have the opportunity to make you self-conscious, faint of heart, or sophisticated.

Although you may be silencing your internal editor, remember to keep a few juggling balls in the air. In particular, write honestly and thoughtfully. Merely recording information will not help you to explore. For example, if you were free-writing about your breakfast, "I ate bacon, eggs, toast, and coffee" would not show much evidence of exploration. Ask yourself why you ate what you did, and why you didn't have café au lait and a croissant. Your next line might then be, "Obviously, I prefer the American variety of cholesterol to the European." As you write, push more deeply into your topic; never use free-writing to produce only superficial information.

When you have finished, review what you have written. Sometimes you will find a good topic sentence for a paragraph that is giving you trouble. Failing that, you are still likely to find that you have managed to see your material in a different way, probably a simpler, clearer way, and your next attempt to write about it formally should be more successful. Always assume, by the way, that whatever you have free-written you must rewrite — not just fine-tune, but "rewrite" as in "rethink."

Peter Elbow has written extensively on free-writing in his books, *Writing Without Teachers* and *Writing With Power*.[3] You may want to consult his texts for further free-writing strategies.

Exercise One: Free-writing

Spend ten minutes free-writing with no particular focus. Simply try to find out what you have in mind at the moment.

Then spend twenty minutes free-writing with a particular focus. If you are working on an essay, one of the following might be a useful focus: the thesis, two ideas that you are having trouble connecting, or possible conclusions for your paper. If not, concentrate your attention on one of the following topics:

1. What you don't want to be when you grow up, and why.

2. Who you would pick for the next Prime Minister.

3. The advantages of knowing a foreign language.

---

[3] See *Writing Without Teachers* (New York: Oxford, 1973); *Writing With Power* (New York: Oxford, 1981).

4. What you do when you write an essay.

Free-Writing a Draft/Reverse Outlines

Sometimes, you will find free-writing for twenty minutes or half an hour unsatisfactory; unstructured composition for such a limited amount of time may not permit you to embrace the full scope of an essay topic. In this situation, you might want to free-write an entire draft of your paper. Provided you take the proper approach, this prewriting strategy is perfectly reasonable.

However, a few cautionary notes are required. Free-writing a rough draft can be very time-consuming; you must battle to ensure that it isn't. Set yourself a time limit. For instance, give yourself one day to write three thousand words, and stop when you have reached that goal. Remember, this is free-writing, not the composition of a first draft. You will still have to write a draft, revise it, and edit it.

Also, be sure to continue to ignore the conventions of essay writing and punctuation; concentrate on understanding your topic. There is no point in revising as you free-write, because you can't know for sure that the sentences you revise will even appear in the draft versions.

Once you have a free draft composed, you should create an outline from it so that you can approach the first draft in an organized fashion. Read over what you have written; glean a thesis from it. Decide what your major points are, what your minor points are, and what will not be used in the essay at all. (The sections omitted may be fairly substantial; do not include passages simply because you have committed them to paper.) Then follow the advice given in the section below to channel your free-writing into an outline.

Outlining

Lily Briscoe, an artist in Virginia Woolf's novel *To the Lighthouse*, describes the qualities she is striving for in her painting this way:

> Beautiful and bright it should be on the surface, feathery and evanescent, one colour melting into another like the colours on a butterfly's wing; but beneath the fabric must be clamped together with bolts of iron. It was to be a thing you could ruffle with your breath; and a thing you could not dislodge with a team of horses.[4]

---

[4] Virginia Woolf, *To the Lighthouse* (Harmondsworth, England: Penguin, 1964) 194.

Like good paintings, good essays are structured so well that they appear to have no structure at all. Inspect any worthwhile essay closely, however, and you will discover, beneath the eloquent prose, the carefully wrought framework that Lily requires of her paintings. It is this framework, in fact, which makes the essay readable, for the proper arrangement of ideas and details is essential to a lucid and persuasive argument. Not all essayists work from outlines, but an essay from which an outline cannot be extracted is more likely to be baffling than brilliant. If the outline is not inherent in the essay, you may be able to fulfill your thesis, but the reader will not be able to discern it.

Many students shy away from essay outlines because they find them confusing and cumbersome, but this reluctance is often the result of a faulty approach. It is difficult — indeed, impossible — to record all the details of an argument at an early stage in the essay; you should not expect to be able to do so. Although a sketchy outline can be constructed almost as soon as a thesis is discovered, an outline expands and develops with reading and research. It is complete only at the moment before drafting begins, and may in fact be revised again if new direction emerges during writing. Think of the outline as something you create over the course of researching and prewriting, and it will be an effective tool.

Outlines are usually understood to be a means of getting organized, and certainly spending some time outlining an essay can be practical and efficient. Ultimately, it will make the writing easier. By having the whole essay condensed on one page, you will be able to see the shape of the whole, the purpose of your paper, the relations between the main points and the supporting details, and the relative weight that should be assigned to each section. The outline therefore serves not only as a guide when you write, but also shows gaps in logic, and indicates whether you need to add or omit information and ideas. In short, an outline organizes not only your writing, but also your thinking. A good outline will establish direction and topic limitation, as well as the order of paragraphs.

Methods of Organization

Eventually, you will want an outline that organizes the actual points and details you wish to include, a place to put all the research you have accumulated. However, an essay is not just a body of information; generally, it has a definite purpose that supplies shape and meaning. Before you begin putting the details of your essay into place, it is useful, therefore, to step back and consider what you are trying to create. Do you want to make a comparison? describe a process? evaluate a report? The location of details will depend on how these questions about general structure are answered. Begin your outline, then, by seeking an organizational framework – a means of considering your material that will convey its purpose clearly.

In the excellent textbook, *Four Worlds of Writing*, Janice Lauer and her co-writers present four different means of organizing ideas in a paper, each suited to a different purpose.[5] We describe these methods below. Consider each method of organization carefully; one will emerge as the most appropriate for the overall arrangement of the particular concept or argument you wish to explore.

Description

Description is a much more analytical act than many textbooks suggest. When we describe, we are, quite literally, analyzing: breaking a whole into parts. For example, when we describe a person's face, we talk about colour of eyes and hair, the shape of the nose and lips, the texture of skin, and the length of eyelashes. That is, we do not talk about the whole, but about the parts which comprise the whole. We might well conclude, however, after we had described the face, that as a whole, it is an attractive one.

The descriptive method of organization in an essay works much the same way. Imagine, for example, that you are writing an essay on the status of women in twentieth-century Canada. Your thesis might be that the status of women in twentieth-century Canada is unacceptable. To prove that point, you would have to analyze the situation by describing the aspects of women's status that led you to such a conclusion. You might write:

The status of women in twentieth-century Canada is unacceptable.
1) It is unacceptable because pay equity hasn't been achieved.
2) It is unacceptable because women are expected to work a double day.
3) It is unacceptable because only a small proportion of women have prestigious jobs.

If your thesis seems to demand that you break an assertion into component parts in order to explain it, then the descriptive method of organization is appropriate for your paper.

---

[5] See Janice Lauer, Gene Montague, Andrea Lunsford, and Janet Emig, *Four Worlds of Writing*, 2nd ed. (New York: Harper and Row, 1985).

Narration

When you organize using the narrative method, the topic is usually being examined in terms of chronology or process. Such a method may seem very elementary, but it can allow you to understand such diverse matters as how the past informs the present, how society can be changed, how the universe unfolds. On a less grand scale, writing about the locomotion of arthropods, for example, might dictate discussing a process, so the narrative method would make sense for this paper. Similarly, writing about the Conservative party in Canada may demand that you consider the party from its roots to its present status to establish how it has developed. Once again, the narrative method, which would permit you to consider the topic of the Conservative party as it moves through time, would be an appropriate method of organization.

Essays on causes and effects often take a narrative form as well. In order to discuss why the Boer War occurred, or what the results of extensive use of non-biodegradables might be, it is necessary to examine the topic over time. A word of caution however: do not confuse narrative development with producing a plot summary or a chronology. The essay must show evidence of your mind at work, selecting the most significant features of the process or discussing how one stage leads to another.

Classification

In an English essay, you might want to consider Stephen Leacock's *Sunshine Sketches* as a satire. The classification method of development, which usually involves putting a subject in a larger group in order to consider it more closely, would work well in this case. To classify, you need to define the larger group (What is a satire?) and then show how Leacock's text shares features with that larger group. (The book is comic; it makes fun of certain aspects of society; it invites the reader to help change those aspects.)

Comparison/contrast essays are a specialized form of classification organization. To compare any two items successfully, the items must belong to the same larger group; otherwise, as the expression goes, you are comparing apples and oranges (not a very useful expression, as you might note, since oranges and apples are both part of the same larger group of fruits).

When you compare, you still place the items in the context of that larger group. However, you will also proceed with an additional step. Once you have established the features both items share with the larger group, you will discuss divergent features as well. For example, were you comparing apples and oranges in terms of marketability, you might note that, although they are both readily available to the North American consumer, the orange is more appealing since its skin is easier to remove and the consumer is therefore less likely to be worried about ingesting chemicals.

Evaluation

The evaluative method of development dictates that you set a standard for your topic, and measure it against that standard. Is the new housing project in your community the best solution to the problem of affordable housing? In order to evaluate, you must decide what the components of the ideal solution to affordable housing would be, and then determine whether the new housing project meets those criteria.

A final point about methods of organization: they operate on the macro, or global, level of essay writing. These methods of organization will provide your essay with an overall framework, but you can and should depart from them within sections of your essay. For example, although you may be writing a classification essay about *Sunshine Sketches,* your essay could still contain a narrative passage describing the events which helped to shape the nature of Leacock's satire.

Exercise Two: Methods of Organization

You are asked to write an essay on the Fathers of Confederation. Invent some possible theses for this topic, and then decide the method of organization most appropriate for developing each thesis.

Repeat the exercise for the following topics.
1. polar bears
2. the writings of Karl Marx
3. Shakespeare's history plays

The Formal Outline

Once you have decided on the general organizing principle your essay will follow, you can begin to think about completing a formal outline. Such a task is not always necessary. Short essays in particular often do not require an extensive outline since their brevity makes it relatively easy to see how details fit together. However, a formal outline does allow for more control in the writing of longer papers.

Any student who has done much reading about essay composition will know that there are almost as many outline schemata as there are essays. Since most of these are based on the same principle, almost any of them can be effective. An outline's usefulness depends not on keyhole or cloud shapes, or on squares and triangles, but on the effective display of a paper's priorities.

Whatever sort of outline is used, it must establish relations between main points and subordinate points, between subordinate points and details, and between all points and the thesis. Above all, the outline must provide a sketch of the development of the thesis, not just a list of headings. It is vastly more useful to the writer if the line of thinking which the essay follows is displayed than if only the ground to be covered is detailed. To be succinct: the outline should reflect the thesis, not just the topic.

The formal essay outline is hierarchical and linear. It depicts the main stages in the development of the essay in their relation to each other and in the order in which they will occur in the essay itself. Its linearity — first this, then this, then this — makes it easy to write from because it matches the linearity of the essay form. The skeleton of a formal outline should look something like this:

Thesis Statement:

    I.
            A.
                    1.
                    2.
    II.
            A.
                    1.
                    2.
            B.
                    1.
                            a.
                                    i.
                                    ii.
                    2.

This outline establishes relations among the ideas in two ways: through a numbering scheme, and through the way in which points are displayed on the page. Related ideas are grouped together under main categories (I and II in the diagram), and within each of these categories, general (A and B) and specific (1 and 2) ideas are recorded. These divisions can be further broken down (a and b; i and ii), although caution should be exercised at this point – too much specificity often only delays the writing of a paper.

The most expedient way of constructing an outline is to decide first what the main divisions of your essay are, then the secondary categories, and then, in turn, the further subdivisions. Your thesis may suggest the main divisions to you; thinking about methods of development will also help. With practice, you will discover that most essays under five thousand words fall naturally into two to four main divisions. An outline that proposes seventeen main divisions signifies that you have not yet found the connections between your ideas, and are veering away from analysis toward the listy, catalogue-style approach.

However rigidly disciplined the outline might seem in format, developing it should be a flexible process. Think of it as the preliminary sketch that a painter makes before committing oils to canvas: use the outline to try to visualize the essay you have in mind but have not yet thought your way through. Try to imagine its basic shape, the order of sections, the organizational method.

As you proceed through your research, keep improving on your outline. You can go through six or eight versions of an outline in very little time, chopping here, adding there, rearranging the whole order until you have the best structure possible. You can plan a nicely-balanced paper by using the left margin for estimating the space-requirements of the various sections of the essay: five hundred words for this major division, two hundred for that minor one, and so on. Indeed, a good deal of planning can be accomplished with a formal outline, but don't allow a plan of action to prevent you from exploring new ideas. Remember that the outline is more useful if you sketch it in pencil than if you carve it in stone.

Creating the Formal Outline

As we have said, an effective outline must display the essay's thesis. To show how thesis is established through outlines, let's consider the example of Sample Essay A. The thesis of the paper might be expressed as "*The Waste Land* ends in a storm of broken images that reflect the whole poem, but fail to give a clear way out of the problems it presents."

98

The main headings of an outline that considered only topic would look something like this:

   I. central image
  II. conflicting images
 III. fragments

A mere list of headings is of very little use. Although it does show the order in which the main points will be put forward, it does not establish the development of the thesis; the student has not declared the point to be made about the central image or the conflicting images or fragments. As a result, these headings will not be particularly helpful in guiding the student's thought during composition. The following outline would be more constructive:

Thesis: *The Waste Land* ends in a storm of broken images that reflect the whole poem, but fail to give a clear way out of the problems it presents.

   I. The central image of the final section is that of the poem: the waste land.
  II. But conflicting images disturb the absoluteness of the poem's despair by introducing some hope for renewal.
 III. Various devices fragment the final section, making any resolution of the plight portrayed seem doubtful.

The statements made for each section of the paper in this outline provide the student not only with direction, but also with perspective. The outline that combines these elements actually depicts the development of the thesis. In the example above, note also that the order of sections is deliberate, and could not be changed without loss. The writer is employing the narrative mode of development here, showing the process by which T.S. Eliot develops meaning through imagery. Once the writer has established that I is true, the stage has been set to show the reader that II is also true, and once the reader accepts II, III becomes more palatable. Each section, in other words, propels the writer (and invites the reader) into the next section by virtue of the organizational method chosen.

This sort of format also can help you to direct your research. The main headings above would be formulated at an early stage in the research process, probably after the student had read *The Waste Land* several times, but before a complete understanding of each image in the poem had been reached. Once aware of the argument to be put forward about the three main points, the student could direct attention toward particular images and changes in the movement of the poem which will help to refine the analysis of the poem as a whole. In this way, the student creates a more detailed outline. Misreadings can also be pointed out in this process. If a particular interpretation of imagery cannot be defended, the lack of supporting detail for it in the essay outline will suggest that it should be eliminated from the argument.

Following is a more fully developed outline of "Images and Gobbledegook: Rain and Doubt in the Final Section of T.S. Eliot's *The Waste Land.*"

Thesis: *The Waste Land* ends in a storm of broken images that reflect the whole poem, but fail to give a clear way out of the problems it presents.

    I. The central image of the final section is that of the whole poem: the waste land.
            1. Title image reflects most of the imagery of the final section.

   II. But conflicting images disturb the absoluteness of the poem's despair by introducing some hope for renewal.
            1. Movement of dryness/water imagery through the section
               a. stanza 1: imagery moves from no hope to possibility of hope (some water imagery) back to no hope; ends with suggestion of hope—"bringing rain"
            2. Portrayal of human nature as locked within ourselves takes poem back toward despair.
               a. can't sympathize (ll. 401-06)
               b. can't communicate—F.H. Bradley (ll. 412-15)
            3. But image of human heart as boat responding gaily to control conflicts with other images that confirm despair.
               a. stanzas 8,9 full of water imagery, both positive and negative: boat imagery versus arid plain over shoulder

  III. Various devices fragment the final section, making any resolution of the plight portrayed seem doubtful.
            1. references to literary works
               a. line from *Purgatorio*
               b. Hindu thunder parable

2. other languages
   a. Modern English prose grabs reader's attention
   b. Hindu words confuse reader
3. London Bridge image in last stanza recalls earlier
   imagery of the (fragmented) urban landscape.
   a. bridge a whole community
   b. falling towers, ruined chapel, etc.

Exercise Three: Creating the Outline

The preceding outline, like most plans that writers work from, is useful but not impeccable as a sketch of the thesis. Ask yourself how it might be polished by considering the following questions: Is it apparent from this outline how the thesis will be demonstrated? Are all section headings written in the form of thesis statements? Is the organizational method apparent and appropriate?

Exercise Four: Creating the Reverse Outline

Do a reverse outline of one of your own essays in linear form. First, look for the thesis statement, then the main divisions of the paper. Include the mini-theses for each main section, and work toward three levels of subdivision (I.A.1). You should end up with a one-page sketch of the argument of the paper. Alternatively, use another student's essay or a published essay for this exercise.

Checking the Formal Outline

Get into the habit of looking for three main qualities in the outline as you refine it: stride, analysis, and substance. These qualities can be verified by a simple visual check—the look of the outline—and they are more easily seen in a formal outline than in a mind-map.

First, stride. Do the main divisions of your thesis move somewhere? You should be taking mental steps from section to section, not inching your way along.

Second, analysis. Say your thesis has three main sections. Ask yourself, "If I show my reader that the mini-thesis for section one is true, and for section two, and for three, will my reader see that my main thesis is true?" Then check within each section in the same sort of way. By this means, you are checking the basic analytical integrity of your thesis.

You are seeing, in other words, whether the pieces into which you have broken your main thesis are the ones needed to reconstruct the whole. If not, either some of the pieces belong to another essay, or your thesis still needs refining. The outline and the thesis must fit together perfectly.

Third, substance. Are your assertions backed up by evidence? Look at the level of your outline which deals with detail. Do you find sufficient reference to your material to back up the assertions you are making about it? You can write a witty, insightful, even elegant essay, but if you do not show your reader how your insights illuminate the material itself, you will not be rewarded for your efforts. You will, in fact, seem more interested in your own cleverness than in the topic you are exploring. While this narcissism is not unknown among academics, being blatant about it in print is a serious *faux pas*. Be sure that your musings are securely rooted in the good earth, and that the reader can see that they are.

Checklist: Outlines

1. **Have you placed your thesis at the top of your outline? Does every main division and every subdivision advance your thesis?**

2. **Does your outline emphasize important ideas and details by giving them adequate space?** Check for gaps and bulges; as a general rule, look for evidence of biting off more than you can chew (too little support, reader getting suspicious), and worse yet, chewing more than you've bitten off (too much support, reader getting sleepy).

3. **Are your details, examples, and more specific statements subordinated to the general statements in the outline?**

4. **Are ideas of the same level of generality ranked equally in your outline?**

5. **Is there a good mix of main headings and subordinate points?** If you find that you are listing a large number of points as main headings, you may not be generalizing enough.

6. **Do your main divisions suggest the direction of your thesis?**

7. **Are the ideas arranged in the most effective order?**

8. **Is your outline concise?** It is important that the outline contain enough detail to enable you to move easily to the first draft; but it must also be brief enough to give you a picture of the whole. If you find that your outline has grown to three pages, write another one-page outline (on foolscap if necessary) to be sure that you are clear about the main lines of your essay.

Exercise Five: Checking the Reverse Outline

Read through the essay on lobby groups in Appendix D; then, complete a reverse outline of it. Does the reverse outline help you to see the structure of the essay? Can you refine the outline? Do you see how the essay might be restructured?

Exercise Six: Checking the Outline

Assess an outline you have produced for an essay of your own. Does it have the qualities of stride, analysis, and substance? Are there gaps or bulges? What changes would you make to the outline if you were to rewrite this paper?

Not employing an outline makes your essay a "high risk endeavour" in one of two ways. Some students go the "work to the deadline" route; they use drafts as outlines and therefore have a tendency to produce an eccentric and misshapen third draft that becomes the final draft because the essay is overdue. Others, slightly less diligent, produce awkwardly structured first drafts that become final versions because they cannot bear to scrap the result of so much work. You may be one of the lucky few who are quite capable of producing an organized paper without benefit of an outline, but if the words "poorly organized" appear anywhere in your instructor's comments, take heed of the suggestions in this section.

Once you have achieved an outline which seems strong and genuinely useful, the process of writing the essay can begin. Try not to write mechanically from the outline; doing so will give your essay a stilted tone and cramp your thinking. If, in the course of writing, a brilliant idea occurs to you that you had not anticipated at the outline stage, cheerfully change your plans. Only be sure to revise the outline, and check that your altered course still gets you where you want to go.

CHAPTER SEVEN
Drafting

The composition process has been described by Ann Berthoff as an act of "making meaning," a turn of phrase that indicates precisely writing's duality of purpose.[1] On the one hand, words are the symbols through which we externalize and shape the process of thought. We think through writing, "making meaning" for ourselves — making sense of our subject, discovering its significance to us. But while writing permits us to explore, it also allows us to communicate — to "make meaning" for a reader. We write to discover what we think, but we also write to tell others what we are thinking.

These dual (and sometimes duelling) purposes figure prominently in the composition of a first draft. At this point, the writer is still in search of meaning. Although one necessarily begins a draft with at least a premise (or hypothesis) and probably a formal outline, in the process of writing one must be allowed the freedom to test and examine and expand, to pursue a natural course of exploration and investigation. The essayist, like the scientific experimenter, must observe the effects of the method employed, both anticipated and unforeseen. Conclusions must arise from the process of wriggling free from the restraints of preconception and prescription even if (and especially if) those conclusions undermine or redirect the tentative thesis or purpose.

At the draft stage, however, the writer will also begin the task of conveying ideas to an audience, and will move away from a personal

---

[1] See Ann Berthoff, *The Making of Meaning: Metaphors, Models and Maxims for Writing Teachers* (Upper Montclair, N.J.: Boynton/Cook, 1981).

and private record of exploration toward a form of writing that "makes meaning" for an unseen reader. Written language, shaped as it is into phrases, sentences, paragraphs, essays, conveys meaning through its organization. The conventions of the introduction and the paragraph, the rules of punctuation and syntax, serve like the movements of dance to choreograph the motion of the mind: they draw patterns of meaning out of our initial, insinuating gestures toward thought by arranging and directing, ordering and scripting chaos. The conventions of written language help thought to emerge from language, just as the choreographer coaxes the dance from the dancer.

The most practical way to view a draft, then, is as an *essai,* an attempt at both thinking and writing about your topic. You will want, in thinking, to get your ideas on paper so that they can be examined, reconsidered, revised. You must therefore write quickly, recording ideas as they occur to you, exploring and refining thought. However, in terms of the finished product, you also want a draft you can work with, a draft that has some meaning: it may have a few tangents, but it should not be entirely tangential; it may depart from your outline, but it needs some semblance of organization.

As far as the thinking is concerned, you are on your own. No guide to essay writing can help you invent your ideas, other than by encouraging you to use writing as an opportunity for exploration. But in this chapter we can help you with the second objective. We will show you how to put together a first version of your essay that will be of use to you when you commence the hard task of revising and truly making meaning for your reader.

Composing The Draft

Before you can grasp the components of a first draft, you must understand how the finished essay works to make meaning for the reader. The key word here is *unity.* To persuade a reader that you understand a topic, you must produce a unified essay, just as a choreographer would labour to ensure that, despite the twenty people moving in different directions on the stage, the audience still perceives the elemental whole of the dance.

Another analogy may help you to see how important unity is. Imagine, for a moment, that you want to establish your understanding of the mechanism of a clock or watch. You begin by disassembling the watch into its component parts. When the watch is in fifty separate pieces on your desk, *you* can see how it operates. But to convince anyone else that you understand the mechanism, you must put the pieces back together, re-fashioning it into a unified, ticking whole. Likewise with an essay. Although "analyze" means to "break into parts," breaking into parts is never enough. You must synthesize as well by reuniting the disparate elements. In this creation of a whole, your understanding of the subject is established.

Creating unity involves not only combining parts to form a whole, but also showing clearly and distinctly the relation between parts. We have all had the experience of watching a rock video in which incongruous elements are juxtaposed; we leave the screen wondering, "Just what was the connection between the attractive woman and the aquarium?" As artists, many video producers deliberately try to evoke the elusive quality of dreams, where the connection between ideas can be guessed at, but not stated with certainty. The intent is often to subvert the world of cohesion and order.

Essays are not videos; when written to form, they are card- carrying members of the world of cohesion and order. Helping your reader to understand how you got from one point to another and why you are writing about what you are writing about is all-important in terms of making meaning. Furthermore, your route of exploration must be one that can be followed easily and that makes logical sense. An undergraduate essay is usually not the place for experiments in narrative technique: stream of consciousness writing and flashbacks are taboo.

By the final draft, then, the relation of the components of the essay to each other and to the paper as a whole should be self-evident and unambiguous: unity should be achieved. However, the student who attempts to produce a unified, cohesive essay in a single attempt often falls victim to that dreaded disease of composition, writer's block. The reason for this lies in the fact that creating unity is not an isolated task, but an ongoing part of the writing process. As we revise and edit our drafts, we work again to establish the relation between parts and whole. Moreover, unity must be achieved on several planes: at the global level of sections and paragraphs, but also at the more local level of sentences and punctuation. To maximize your ability to explore while still creating a piece of work that will be useful to you, contemplate unity as you draft, but only at the global level, at the level of the sections and paragraphs of the essay. Considerations are broader here, but they are also less numerous, so the flow of your writing (and the activity in your mind) will be less inhibited than if you worried about word choice, punctuation, and tone. Because one begins writing with words and sentences, thinking about them too much during drafting can keep a writer stuck forever on the first paragraph. Better to give some thought to sections: that way, you can hold the essay in your mind and you have an approach that propels you forward, rather than leaving you beached on page one.

A final gentle reminder before you begin: relax. Give some thought to what follows, but do not aim now for a completely unified product, even at the global level. Remember, as well, that although "making meaning" for a reader is important, you should also be discovering meaning for yourself at this point. Don't concentrate on unity so rigidly that you forget to think deeply about your subject.

Part One: The Sections

Very few essays, no matter what their thesis, cannot be subdivided into major sections. As we consider a topic, we almost automatically break it into pieces of accessible size. For instance, a student writing on the vegetation in a particular area would certainly devise some categories in which to place ideas – trees, flowers, fruits, and vegetables, perhaps, or spring, summer, and fall vegetation. The reader, likewise, prefers demarcated sections; information is more easily retained when perused in manageable chunks. Since sections serve both the writer and the reader, you should think while you draft about what they are and how they relate to each other. In terms of the content in your paper, you will find that the way you arrange ideas into sections can help your reader understand your material better. In addition, you will discover that certain sections of the essay – the introduction, conclusion, and transitional sections – have as their primary function the task of helping the reader realize the unity of a paper.

Methods of Organization

If you have produced a formal outline for your essay, you will already have contemplated unity at the section level: the methods of development discussed in the chapter on prewriting – description, narration, classification, and evaluation – are means of showing how sections of a paper are related to one another. Using a particular method to establish the connections between the sections of your essay will make it easier for both you and your reader to predict what comes next and to fit the sections together.

Most theses can be developed according to any one of the four organizational methods: your choice should be based on which fits your thesis best. For example, if your topic were the dangers of nuclear energy, each of the methods would be a possibility. Were you trying to argue that nuclear energy stations should be abolished, you might use the descriptive method, articulating the reasons why these stations are dangerous. If your intent is to show how the dangers of these stations have increased since World War II, a narrative method would be appropriate. You might, on the other hand, be arguing that nuclear stations aren't nearly as dangerous as coal mines, and the classification method would work well then. Finally, if you were trying to establish the strengths and weaknesses of nuclear energy, you might use the evaluative method, envisioning what the ideal energy supply would be and judging nuclear energy against that standard.

No matter what method of organization you select, remember that it need organize only the sections of your paper; it is not necessary to maintain the same organizational approach within sections.

Rhetorical Strategies

Once you have decided on an organizational method, you will have sections, but a decision may need to be made about the arrangement of those sections. This decision is a rhetorical one in that you choose the most persuasive arrangement of your ideas. Rhetorical strategies provide unity by giving the writer another means of establishing how ideas fit together; used effectively, they can allow you to demonstrate your sense of what the reader should see as primary, secondary, or tangential.

Rhetorical and organizational strategies work together to make meaning. One need not override the other. For instance, let's return to the descriptive organization of the dangers of nuclear power. You know you will talk about three dangers, but which one should come first? The answer lies in a consideration of rhetorical arrangement. The following examples of common rhetorical methods illustrate different possibilities for the arrangement of sections and the effect each creates.

1. *General to Specific*
   The topic is approached on a general level first, and more specific details follow. Were your topic the dangers of nuclear energy, you could begin by discussing the problems caused by radiation in general, and then discuss the particular dangers present within a nuclear power station. Using this arrangement can help you to maintain your focus throughout.

2. *Specific to General*

Here, the details appear before the more general comments. You would commence by discussing specific health hazards faced by Darlington workers, and finish by considering the broader environmental implications of nuclear energy. The rhetorical advantage is that the generalizations seem inevitable by the time you make them; the disadvantage is that it is more difficult to maintain and control your focus if you arrange your ideas in this way. You must be sure that the specifics have an intrinsic interest, that you do not confuse and consequently irritate your reader, and that the conclusion gains from being held in suspense.

3. *Climax*

The points appear in order of least to most important to the argument. For instance, if you consider the day-to-day hazards in a nuclear plant more dangerous to workers than the very unlikely possibility of a nuclear explosion, you might choose to deal with explosions first. Your intent must be clear to the reader from the outset when a climactic arrangement is used; otherwise, the ideas presented will only confuse.

4. *Increasing Complexity*

A variation on the climactic model, this pattern arranges points from the simplest to the most complex. Since you begin by establishing those points which it is easiest to prove, this arrangement allows you to advance your argument relatively quickly and thereby establish a strong momentum early in the essay. In an essay on nuclear plants, your simplest point would probably be the consequences of a nuclear explosion, since they are obvious and drastic. You could begin there and work through to more intricate and pernicious problems.

Many well-organized essays are written without a deliberate application of these methods of organizing material. However, it is useful to be familiar with them. Consider the variety of methods of development and rhetorical arrangements possible when you are wondering where to start and which section to write next, and include arrangement of ideas among the qualities you check for when you are revising the first draft.

Introductions, Transitional Paragraphs, and Conclusions

Another objective in drafting is to consolidate ideas, and particular sections of the essay focus almost entirely on this goal. Introductions can begin to achieve unity by preparing the reader for the sections which follow. Well-written transitional paragraphs, which announce and explain a shift in thought process, will provide unity within the body of the paper. Conclusions, if they refresh the reader's mind about purpose and implications, can augment unity where it counts most: at the end of the paper, when the reader is also drawing conclusions about the effectiveness of the essay.

Introductions

Probably more paper gets thrown in the recycling bin when writers are attempting introductions than at any other time. Getting those first few paragraphs down can take Herculean effort; we hesitate because we are appalled by the magnitude and difficulty of the task before us, and we fear that unless we find exactly the right way to begin, we will botch the job entirely. Fear and loathing and basic laziness aside, we are usually not very good when we begin a new piece, often because we are unsure where we are going.

Eventually, your introduction will become the key to your essay: by reading it, the reader will be thoroughly prepared for the maze of intellectual and creative thought about to be experienced. But when you haven't gone on the journey yet, it is fairly difficult to map where you have been. If you are unable to produce a creative introduction the first time around, use your initial effort to help maintain unity through the draft. You know your major sections: outline what they are and how you intend to consider them.

Then, move on to the body of the essay. There is little point trying to achieve a creative introduction in the first draft if one doesn't occur to you easily; through the writing process, you may move away from your initial intent and have to revise all those clever turns of phrase anyway. What you want at this stage is a working introduction, one that will keep your draft intact but that does not drain all your creative energy in its production.

Transitional Paragraphs

Once you begin drafting the body of your paper, you have started an exploratory journey that can lead you into all sorts of quagmires, animal traps, and enchanted forests. Some of these will prove to be worthwhile and valuable digressions, but you must keep your initial task in mind: get that dragon slain. Otherwise, overall unity will disintegrate.

One sound way of maintaining this unity is through the use of transitional paragraphs. When you have finished a section of your paper, pause in the production of content and use a paragraph to regroup your thoughts. Discuss what you have written and what you are going to write; decide on the connection between the two. Because such paragraphs force you to consider more carefully the direction you are taking, they are useful in, perhaps even essential to, the composing process. (Are you getting any closer to the damsel in distress?) Also, if they are strategically placed between each of the major sections of your paper, they keep your reader aware of your thesis and its development.

Begin each transitional paragraph by summing up the section you have just written, elaborating on its significance to your paper. Then, explain to your reader and yourself how it connects to what will follow. Is the next section more important? Less important? Does it develop an idea further? Conclude the transitional paragraph by introducing the next section of your paper; name what is to follow.

Paragraph #7 in Sample Essay C establishes what a handy writing tool the transitional paragraph can be. The student has finished discussing how the disease affecting the harbour seals was identified; now, the essay needs to move forward to the matter of understanding the origin of the disease. The material about identification is summarized, but the student then informs the reader that identification is only the beginning of the situation; scientists need also to understand the origins of the disease and the reasons for the seals contracting it.

Conclusions

By the time you are concluding your first draft, you probably will have begun to realize the route of exploration your paper has taken. This route may be the one you foresaw in your outline, or it may diverge slightly from it. In the process of writing, for example, you might discover that two ideas you thought unrelated have strong parallels. If these parallels are worth investigating, do not eliminate them simply because they do not match a preconceived thesis. Rather, make a note to revise your thesis in order to include the new points.

Eventually, your conclusion will serve to unify the entire paper, pulling together the ideas contained, pointing out their implications. In a first draft, try to get at the bare bones of that unity. Think seriously about what you have written thus far, about the substance of each section, and summarize what it all means. Don't worry too much about grand rhetorical flourishes; if those are necessary, there will be plenty of opportunity to invent them at the revision stage. What you want now is a sturdy conclusion that permits you to understand what you have written, one that can act as a guide at the level of global revision.

Part Two: The Paragraph

Thinking about sections provides a bird's eye view of the essay, but when we are actually writing, it is often hard to see the whole enchanted forest: the trees of content keep getting in the way. As you produce a first draft, then, you need not only think about the essay as a broad whole – about the larger sections – but also about how meaning is made from the bottom up, about how the smaller parts fit together to produce the essay.

If the sections of an essay provide meaning by dividing the thesis into easily understood components, then the paragraph can be seen as developing bits of ideas into units large enough to make meaning clear. The paragraph is the basic unit of essay composition; it is like a little essay in itself. Taken together, all of the paragraphs in the essay are a visual representation of the thinking process by which the writer demonstrates his or her thesis.

As with sections, therefore, the principles of unity emerge as crucial. Each paragraph must be a unified entity; that is, it must be about only one main idea. Furthermore, the main idea must be developed through details, examples, and explanations so that the reader can see how the sentences within the paragraph form that entity. Finally, there must be connections made both within and between paragraphs so that the reader can move easily through one paragraph and on to the next. Do not expect your paragraphs to meet all of these criteria in a first draft. In the revision process, you will have plenty of opportunity to tighten cohesion and to make a paragraph more unified. For the time being, just consider the following general information about paragraphs and try to apply it. Do not, however, focus on paragraphs to the extent that you curtail the free flow of your thought.

The Controlling Idea

The paragraph develops one small idea just as the essay develops one large idea, and each new paragraph signals a shift in focus, whether in time or place, in approach, in subject, or in idea. Thus, a paragraph break does more than give the reader a little rest; it allows both reader and writer to see the structure of the essay.

What a paragraph needs, therefore, is a controlling idea – a principle or concept that dictates the content of the passage. Quite simply, you should be able to sum up in one sentence what a paragraph is about. The summation need not actually be a part of the paragraph (we refer to it as a topic sentence when it is), but all sentences in the paragraph should have a direct connection to it. For example, the controlling idea of this paragraph is the definition of a controlling idea.

Developing the Controlling Idea

A controlling idea will help you achieve a unified paragraph, but developing that idea is also important. A controlling idea on its own does not constitute a paragraph: it needs to be fleshed out with relevant details, examples, implications, and qualifications. If paragraphs were not developed in this way, writers would run through their general ideas like soothsayers in such a hurry to proclaim their wisdom that they have no time to be interesting, clear, or persuasive.

A paragraph in an academic essay, therefore, is rarely only one or two sentences (although such short passages may be used occasionally to summarize, emphasize, or provide a transition from one main idea to the next). About one hundred to two hundred words is a more appropriate length in terms of development.[2]

Making Connections Clear

Since each new paragraph signals a change in focus, each is a potential source for lack of cohesion in the essay. Strive as you write to make clear how each paragraph connects to its predecessor. If you fail to do this, you cannot expect the reader to make these connections: you may find, when your essay is returned, that you have been misinterpreted.

Internally, paragraphs must also move smoothly from one idea to the next; the reader should be able to see how each sentence relates to the controlling idea and to the other sentences around it. In other words, the paragraph must advance the main idea without losing the reader; it must have an internal cohesion.

Another aspect of connecting ideas within paragraphs is connecting your own prose to the prose you quote: incorporating quotations. Many students display anti-social mannerisms in their style of quotation.

---

[2] You will notice that many of the paragraphs in this text are very short. We consciously chose small controlling ideas so that our readers would not have to work too hard to understand each point. The controlling idea of an essay paragraph, however, can be much larger than those in the paragraphs of *Thinking It Through*.

Instead of deftly taking up a pointed phrase into the bosom of their own prose, or off-setting a longer passage the better to focus on it in comments that precede and follow, they stick a colon at the end of a sentence, slap the quotation down like Khrushchev's shoe and say no more about it, as though the gesture, being a crude one, speaks for itself.

The whole point of quotation is not to stack up evidence, courtroom style, but to establish for your reader that in writing your paper, you are engaging in a scholarly debate. Your intent is not to quote authorities but to show the reader that you have listened to them and that you feel that they often have worthwhile things to say. It is your voice the reader should hear, but within your paper that voice should be speaking to the other voices, the other authorities on the topic.

To achieve this dialogue, you must incorporate quotations into your own prose. Introduce the quotation by letting the reader know your opinion of it: do you agree? disagree? feel the author is only partially correct? feel that this example of poetic diction is exemplary? After the quotation has been recorded, comment further by telling the reader what was significant in the passage quoted. Draw attention to the particular phrase or idea you wish the reader to see in the passage. The aim, once again, is internal unity: ensure that your quotation works with the rest of the paragraph to create a unified whole.

You may realize by now that this chapter on writing differs from the others in *Thinking It Through* in that it contains no checklists or exercises. These omissions are deliberate. As we wrote in the introduction to this chapter, a first draft is an attempt at an essay, not something that can be considered complete, or something that can be made perfect with practice. Inevitably, the draft will fall short in some ways: the organization is weak, or the transitional paragraphs are missing, or the paper has a thesis in the body other than the one stated in the introduction. These imperfections should not concern you during drafting. You can save extensive deliberations for revision: at this stage, roll up your sleeves, repeat your mantra, and write.

Revising and Proofreading

Part One: Revising

The ultimate aim in essay writing is to produce prose in which meaning is clear, both to the writer and to the reader. However, it is often impossible for writers to know exactly what they mean until they see what they have written, and this is why revision is such an important aspect of the writing process. Imagine an argument in which you were not allowed to retract or recast a thought, or a first draft that was not full of scratched-out words and inserted phrases. Difficult, isn't it? Because creative people constantly evaluate and reconstruct their ideas and their expressions of ideas, writing inevitably incorporates revision.

Sometimes, it is best to separate these two acts artificially, to put off the assessment and reworking of writing until after a first draft is complete. If you continually rethink every thought before recording it, or if you struggle to achieve clear and graceful language in a first draft, you run the risk of writing very little. So, write the first draft quickly if you can, leaving yourself time to revise carefully after putting it aside for a day or two. With the passage of time, it will be much easier to see your writing as another reader would see it. Also, you will be more likely to see what you actually wrote instead of what you meant to write with the benefit of the distance that a few days can provide.

Above all, remember that you should not feel that you are a failure if you need to rework your first draft. The best writers revise their work constantly, although students often find this difficult to believe. To most of us, good writing seems to have sprung from the writer's mind fully formed; it appears too natural, too obvious and graceful to have been achieved through the process of revision. However, seemingly effortless prose, like seemingly effortless dance, is rarely just that; the easier the performance appears, the harder the performer has worked. Revision is the way a writer works at his or her writing.

When discouraged about your own "natural" ability as a writer, remember that many great writers could more accurately be called great revisors. George Orwell's brother-in-law, with a disrespect common among relatives and close friends, attributed Orwell's success as a writer to hard work, not to talent. As he said, "You can't put in all that amount of work and not get somewhere."[1]

Actually, the act of revising should make you feel powerful and in control of your writing. While your first draft was an attempt to make meaning that was guided only by your outline or by your creative vision, your revised essay is built on your own writing; each revision of this writing should bring you closer to your intentions. While convinced of this fact, a student might still be confused about how to begin revising an essay. To revise a paper means "to look again" at the essay you have made, not just to tinker with what you now have on paper. But what are you looking for? You are looking for discrepancies, discrepancies between what you intended to write and what you actually wrote, between what your audience expects and what you actually deliver. It is wise to look for these discrepancies by examining the whole of your essay before its parts. Revising at the global level first will prevent you from merely changing particularly glaring errors and help you to truly "re-see" your work. Next, your essay's sections should be scrutinized: the paragraphs, the introduction and conclusion. Do these sections work together to create a coherent and cohesive unity? Finally, revise the sentences of your paper so that their syntax, diction, and grammar adequately communicate your ideas.

Revising the Whole

As with drafting, revision begins by considering the global level of your essay: its topic, thesis, and organization; the voice you have used to present your ideas.

---

[1] Audrey Coppard and Bernard Crick, *Orwell Remembered* (London: British Broadcasting Corporation, 1984) 129.

Revising for Topic, Thesis, and Organization

First read the draft in its entirety, pretending that you had no hand in its production. Determine what the topic of the essay is, and see if this topic has been focused on quickly enough. Decide what the main point or thesis of the essay is. It is not sufficient simply to restate your original intentions regarding topic and thesis at this point, since you may have diverged from them. You must try to see and judge your essay as a stranger would. This objective view can be achieved in several ways, all of which require that you ask yourself what the essay really amounts to. Producing a reverse outline could help you see the essay's structure and thesis clearly. You might imagine you are describing the essay to a friend. You could try to think of a situation, event, or thing that exemplifies the central concern of the paper and then test your expression of topic and thesis against this example. Writing a paragraph of three sentences beginning "What this essay is really trying to get across" might also prove useful.

Once you have decided what your first draft is actually about, what its main thrust is and what it veers toward, you have to decide if its direction is appropriate. First of all, are you satisfied with the essay's topic and emphasis? Secondly, does its focus adequately meet the expectations of your instructor or of your writing assignment? Finally, examine the essay's main point and ask yourself what the significance of that point is. Does the whole essay leave you asking "So what?" If so, the essay's topic or thesis needs revision. Even if your essay does answer this question implicitly, ensure that, at some point, it answers it explicitly.

After assessing the significance and appropriateness of the essay's topic and thesis, look to see that these components are clearly expressed and developed. Inexperienced writers seem to digress because they fail to show how the details they recount relate to their papers' major concerns. Make sure that everything in your essay is connected to your topic and advances your thesis. Also, guard against wandering away from your topic and providing your reader with irrelevant information. While you should present all relevant facts and theories adequately and fairly, all that you present must be related to your essay's particular focus. Every general statement you make, including your thesis statement, should be both supported by evidence and connected with the essay as a whole.

If the first stage of revising at the global level involves looking at an essay's topic and thesis, the second stage should include a detailed evaluation of the paper's organization. Now is the time to recall what the chapters on prewriting and drafting taught you about methods of organization and rhetorical strategies. You should examine your essay to see if its underlying outline is suitable and apparent. Check your reverse outline against your original outline, if you produced one, and against your draft to see what omissions or additions you made. Describe the organization of your first draft and ask yourself if a different organization might suit your purpose better. Finally, be sure that your use of transitions and key terms reveals your essay's pattern of development.

Revising for Voice

Every writer strives to find a recognizable and representative voice, a unique style and tone that adequately reflects self. Struggling to achieve this worthy ambition may take a lifetime, but even a novice writer can revise his or her voice so that it is consistent and conforms to the expectations of the academy.

To determine whether you have written your first draft using a consistent voice, read the whole essay aloud (or ask a friend to read it to you). Do you sound like a cheerleader in one section, a skeptic in another, and a fence sitter in the next? Does your prose vacillate between familiarity and remoteness, casualness and formality, or between nonchalant humour at one point and sedate serious-mindedness at another? How do you treat your reader; is it with a mixture of fawning flattery and condescending sarcasm? Obviously, these possible inconsistencies in voice have been exaggerated, but most writers, especially when they are working on an unfamiliar writing task, find it difficult to achieve a regular, harmonious style and tone.

Revising with an eye to the suitability of voice dictates making judgements about audience and purpose. If your purpose is to write an expository essay describing a particular event, circumstance, or process, you would probably lean toward an accurate, unambiguous style and a formal tone. It is hard to imagine a playful, personal voice in an essay on the formation of coral reefs, although such a voice might be entirely appropriate for a paper on the role of the cartoon hero in Canadian cultural mythology. A writer whose main purpose is to persuade might also attempt a closer relationship with the reader by using a more familiar tone. In all cases, the decision to use a less formal voice should be made after considering whether the intended audience would be open to such informality.

Decisions about what readers might consider appropriate are often difficult for students to make. Generally, assume that you are writing for an informed scholarly audience composed of your classmates and your instructor. You must awaken this audience's intellectual curiosity, and you must, at least, make an attempt to meet the conventions of scholarly discourse. What are these conventions? Well, they are constantly changing which makes them hard to define. But they all can be listed as choices that essay writers must make at the global level of revision: whether to use the first and second person ("you" and "I"), gender-neutral language, the active or the passive voice, the "historical present."

You and I

It has been customary in academic work to avoid acknowledging the fact that the writer is an individual (I) speaking to another individual (you), (Hi, there!) as though the admission would somehow threaten the intellectual tone of the work. However problematic that logic, there are two good reasons for honouring the tradition:

1. The whole essay is yours, which means that whenever you say "I feel" your readers might wonder whether you have more or less confidence in this statement than in any other in the essay. They might even think that a statement qualified in this way is a subjective article of faith, not reason.

2. It is risky to address the reader directly. Readers accustomed to a more formal relationship with their writers find "you" overly familiar — the equivalent of the French *tu* when *vous* is prescribed by the social code. The practice is especially objectionable when the writer is presuming the nature of the reader's response: "When you read Lady Macbeth's lines in the sleep-walking scene, you want to cry your heart out." Such presumption is to be avoided no matter what the conventions of your discipline regarding "you" and "I." In this book, for example, we have opted for the familiar "you," but have tried to avoid the presumptuous one.

There are times, however, when it is natural and sensible to use the first person: to make a transition from reporting someone else's thought to asserting your own, or to modulate the force of a piece of writing, whether to tone it down or to make it more assertive. "Although Hobson's analysis is intelligent, I would maintain that his premise is wrong." The only use of "I" that must be strictly avoided is to disguise a weak point:

"Despite the position of most of the human population to the contrary, I feel that the world is flat." Look in recently published journals of your discipline to check on whether and how the first and second person are used. New disciplines have challenged many of the traditional academic conventions, and it may be perfectly legitimate to write certain kinds of essays using "you" and "I." When in doubt, however, avoid both.

Gender-Neutral Language

Writing practices regarding the use of male terms as generics reflective of both men and women have been challenged and changed. The argument that "he" is generic, not male, that "he" means "he or she" already, is no longer acceptable to many academics. These scholars argue that the word "man" does not mean both man and woman, that "policeman" does not mean policewoman too, and that the body of paperboy does not contain the rib that is a papergirl. They feel that "he" does not imply "she too, of course": the image that comes quite sensibly to their minds is incorrigibly, persistently male. In fact, studies indicate that "the pronoun *he* and the noun *man* and its compounds occur much more frequently as sex-specific or ambiguous expressions than as true generics."[2] These studies suggest that the tradition of using male words as generics is inaccurate and in need of reform.

Some professors and writers, however, argue against the use of cumbersome gender-neutral language. They believe that regardless of how well-intentioned linguistic devices which include women might be, some are unnatural, unlovely, and an assault on the elegance of the English language. Especially offensive to their ears and eyes are alternative forms requiring slashes or parentheses like s/he, (s)he, he(she), and him/her.[3] These forms do look and sound awkward because they have no clear counterpart in spoken language. However, is it not better to be ungraceful than unjust?

Can the real concerns of both groups be reconciled? Yes, prose can be revised to demonstrate gender accurately, inoffensively, and elegantly. First of all, however, avoid the generic use of "he" and "man" where such a use is unjust, incongruous, ambiguous, or unacceptable

---

[2] Francine Wattman Frank and Paula A. Treichler, *Language, Gender, and Professional Writing: Theoretical Approaches and Guidelines for Nonsexist Usage* (New York: Modern Language Association of America, 1989) 146.

[3] Indeed, some of our colleagues have argued so convincingly against these particular constructions that this revised edition of *Thinking It Through* does not use them.

to your audience. The social sciences and the sciences have generally adopted the female-inclusive forms of pronouns to enhance the accuracy with which research in these fields can be communicated. If a physical anthropologist is writing about a Palaeolithic female skeleton, for example, precision would dictate the use of the female singular personal pronoun. Also, it would be ridiculous to refer to such a skeleton as an excellent specimen of Neanderthal man. In other disciplines, the practice of including women is preferred by some scholars, acceptable to most, and reviled by a few. Check the journals.

There are many strategies which include women in the English language without offending the grace or elegance of prose. When writing about a person who may be a woman or a man, you could simply use "he or she" or "she or he." Try not to repeat these combinations too frequently, however, as a page littered with such phrases is often difficult to read and too general in tone. The use of double pronouns should also be avoided when revising a sentence liberally peppered with singular pronouns. The following sentence would be an ungainly thing indeed if revised in this way: "He must admit his thievery and show himself reformed before we trust him again with earwigs that are not his." In such cases, rewrite the sentence to cut down on the incidence of pronouns. Voilà: "The thief will neither regain our trust nor touch our earwigs except by admitting guilt and proving reform."

Another option is to alternate masculine and feminine pronouns, using "she" occasionally and "he" at other times. Care must be taken that this strategy does not confuse your reader and that your alternating use of "he" and "she" does not accidentally display sexual stereotypes. It would be embarrassing indeed if you used this option in an attempt to be even-handed and discovered that you had referred to nurses, teachers, and librarians as females and to doctors, professors, and entrepreneurs as males. As a matter of interest, the handbook that many of our parents reared us by, *Dr. Spock's Baby and Child Care,* has been newly revised using this strategy to avoid sexist language.

Sometimes it is possible to revise sentences that use the generic "he" by recasting them into the plural. Since "they," "them," "their," and "themselves" are not sex-specific, this type of revision allows for gender-neutral language. The sentence "A writer must examine his heart to determine if his prose is honest" would become "Writers must examine their hearts to determine if their prose is honest." It can be dangerous to revise in this way if your sentence contains more than one plural noun. Ambiguity of pronoun reference could result. In the following sentence, "they" could refer either to "people" or to "doctors and nurses." "People schooled in the ways of doctors and nurses know that they can cope in a hospital setting." Also, make sure that you do not violate current grammatical logic by referring to singular nouns using plural pronouns.

Another alternative is to revise your sentences so that you use the impersonal pronoun "one," the first person pronouns "I" and "we," or the second person pronoun "you." Considerations of your purpose and of the formality of your writing task should determine which pronoun is most appropriate. You have already been warned of the dangers of using "you" and "I" in academic prose. The only reason to shun the use of "one" is that it might make your writing seem overly formal and stuffy. Any of these pronouns, however, allow you to avoid using the generic "he."

Regardless of the objections of some to the use of gender-neutral language, you probably should revise your writing with an eye to eliminating sexist nouns and pronouns. Barring a return to the days when universities were for men only, we can assume that most scholars will eventually accept "her" on the page beside "him"; after all, they got used to seeing her in the classroom beside him.

Exercise One: Gender-Neutral Language

Revise the following two passages so that women are included in the language used.

1. Narcissism represents the psychological dimension of this dependence. Notwithstanding his occasional illusions of omnipotence, the narcissist depends on others to validate his self-esteem. He cannot live without an admiring audience. His apparent freedom from family ties and institutional constraints does not free him to stand alone or to glory in his individuality. On the contrary, it contributes to his insecurity, which he can overcome only by seeing his "grandiose self" reflected in the attentions of others, or by attaching himself to those who radiate celebrity, power, and charisma. For the narcissist, the world is a mirror, whereas the rugged individualist saw it as an empty wilderness to be shaped to his own design.[4]

---

[4] Christopher Lasch, *The Culture of Narcissism: American Life in An Age of Diminishing Expectations* (New York: W.W. Norton, 1979) 10.

2. Being read fairy tales by a parent is one of the most enriching experiences in childhood. First, the mere presence of a parent is important. Reading is one of many ways in which special moments can be shared with the very young child. More important than the physical presence of the parent is his role as mediator between the child and the fairy story. A mother or father makes a child feel safe in the presence of giants, hungry wolves, and wicked stepsisters. Yet there is an even more subtle kind of reassurance given to the child by the reading parent. Psychologists tell us that the basis of most fears in early childhood is the child's emerging independence from, and subsequent guilt about, his parents. By being present as the child imaginatively kills off wicked stepmothers and replaces them with Prince Charmings, a parent can indicate to a child that he may freely indulge in his fantasies of independence. The child can be assured that his mother or father will survive his aggressive fantasies, and respond to his simultaneous need to be dependent.

Active/Passive Voice[5]

The matter of using active or passive verbs is a less contentious scholarly concern that involves a writer's voice. Most instructors agree that students should maintain an active voice in their essays except in circumstances where the passive is more graceful or meaningful. Such an unusual consensus has probably been reached because there is agreement as to the importance of verbs in making meaning.

The control and imaginative manipulation of verbs is the key to discovering and communicating meaning, to moving a sentence forward toward its purpose. Verbs, not nouns, develop ideas because verbs make, while nouns merely describe. Verbs move, while nouns stand still. Verbs predicate (declare, proclaim, assert) and predication always involves action and movement.

One might say that each verb is a "thesis statement," the impulse of the sentence it generates. The more forceful, the more clear, the more graphic and dynamic the predicate, the more impact it imparts, and consequently the more noticeably it advances the argument of the essay. For that reason the active generally surpasses the passive voice in

---

[5] Verbs that express action originating with a "doer" and affecting someone or something else are called transitive. These transitive verbs have two voices: the active and the passive. In the active voice, the "doer" is the subject of the sentence: "The cow jumped over the moon." In the passive voice, the subject of the sentence is the person or thing affected by the action expressed by the verb, not the "doer" of this action: "The moon was jumped over by the cow."

rhetorical effectiveness. There will be times when a passive is useful or unavoidable, but in the English language a formal argument is best supported and advanced by active verbs.

There are two simple reasons for this preference. First, since the essay is ultimately forward moving, expansive rather than contractive by design, the active voice is the natural key for coherence in composition. The subject moves through the verb toward the object in the active voice (girl shovelled gravel) as opposed to the verb-toward-subject movement of the passive (gravel was shovelled by girl). The active construct, then, steps forward while the passive steps back; and, in the most literal sense, object(ive)s are ordinarily achieved by advance, not retreat. Then, too, the passive construction is built on the past participle of the verb, and so always seems less immediate than the active form. Even in the present tense it seems locked in the past, and heading the wrong way. Consider the effect of the passive on this little treasure from the glamorous lives of the literati:

> Carson McCullers vomits on Tennessee Williams.
> Tennessee Williams is vomited on by Carson McCullers.

This example also demonstrates a further superiority of the active predicate. Because it is less dependent upon prepositions ("by") and auxiliaries ("is"), the active employs fewer words with the obvious consequence that there is less displacement of energy.

The passive is the language of the bureaucrat, the prevaricator, and the accused under cross-examination because it allows for the utterance of complete sentences without naming the agent of the actions described. Only two of the three elements that make up most actions on this planet need be identified when we use the passive voice: the action and the acted upon. The actor may remain nameless. In the following passive construction, we know what is done, and to whom it is done, but Carson McCullers is off the hook:

> Tennessee Williams is vomited on.

Ethically and architectonically, the active predicate is altogether the simpler, stronger, and more attractive structure; by moving the reader forward, it provides a coherence that the passive cannot achieve.

The active, too, presents the reader with a bolder, more vividly and immediately imaginable picture of what the writer wants to say. And any written expression that offers the reader access to the imagination in the pursuit of logic is rhetorically preferable to a wordy abstraction.

For these reasons, it is wise to revise your first draft so that all of your verbs are as powerful and active as you can make them. It is very easy to slip into the passive voice when you are trying to be objective. The active voice tends to name names. Sometimes this directness, clarity, and assurance frightens writers who are unused to composing essays and unsure of the value of their written contributions. They prefer to write evasively because of these insecurities. Nevertheless, these writers should take courage and write actively. An equivocal essay is usually judged more harshly than one written in a direct and clear manner.

The Historical Present

Instructors also generally agree that students should use the "historical present" when describing events in a work of literature or when discussing the intent and impact of long-dead authors. It is more accurate to use the present tense in these circumstances because the arguments put forward by scholars, the characters presented and the scenes depicted by novelists, poets, and dramatists continue to live in the present. An added benefit is that the use of the present tense makes for immediate and lively writing.

Consider how dull Sample Essay A would sound if its author did not use the "historical present" frequently in references made to Eliot's work. If the essay had been written using the past tense, this excerpt would read as follows:

> The poem *presented* fragmented scenes of a purposeless, empty existence with no hope of renewal or resurrection. In the final section, as one *might have hoped*, T.S. Eliot *talked* about the rain that could bring relief to this waste land. Yet the Hindu thunder proverb that he *offered was* alien enough to a Western reader that this resurrection *seemed* almost forced or artificial. The poem *ended* in a storm of broken images that *reflected* the whole poem, but *failed to give* a clear way out of the problems it *presented*.

Compare the passage above to the original version. Do you notice how direct and clear the original is? In the rewritten version, the past tense renders the analysis remote and ineffective. Check your draft to see that you have employed the "historical present" whenever its use brings strength and immediacy to your voice.

Exercise Two: The Historical Present

Examine the three sample essays and pinpoint examples of the use of the "historical present." Recast some of these passages into the past tense. Compare these revised passages to the originals and contrast the effectiveness of each. While you are working, check the sample essays for instances where the "historical present" might have been used but was not.

Checklist: Revising the Whole

Topic and Thesis

1. What is the essay about? What is its topic and its central concern or thesis?

2. How significant is the essay? Have you demonstrated this significance?

3. Does the essay's topic and focus fulfill the expectations of the audience?

4. What promises does the essay make to its readers? Are these promises kept?

5. Is the purpose or the thesis of your essay stated clearly and developed sufficiently?

6. Does everything in your essay relate to your topic and thesis, and have you demonstrated these relations?

7. Have you provided sufficient and accurate facts, references, quotations, examples, and illustrations to support your thesis and all other general statements?

8. Have you commented on how the evidence you provide is significant to the development of your essay?

Organization

1. How is your essay organized?

2. Will the pattern by which your essay develops be clear to a reader? Can you underline specific words and passages in your paper that help a reader see this pattern?

3. Would a different rhetorical or organizational strategy suit your purpose better?

4. Do you indicate which ideas are of major importance and give these ideas proper emphasis?

5. Are there gaps in the logical development of your essay which need to be filled? Are there intrusions which sidetrack the main thrust of your paper that should be removed or rearranged?

6. Have you used transitions to show the relations between the points you make?

Voice

1. Have you maintained the same voice throughout the essay? Try to personify this voice. Does it suggest that of a particular type of person? Who?

2. Are you the person you want to be in this essay? Do you sound authentic? Would a different voice suit your purpose or your audience better?

3. Is your writing overly formal or informal? Do you use "you," "I," "we," and "one" appropriately?

4. Will the way you have referred to gender please or offend your audience? Did you follow the conventions of your discipline when deciding how to use gender-neutral language?

5. Have you used the active voice as much as is suitable? Are your verbs expressive and strong?

6. Have you used the "historical present" when discussing scholarly works and when describing the events recounted in literature? Is your voice immediate and direct?

Revising the Sections

By now, you should have a good grasp of your essay's overall purpose, structure, and voice. With the most global revisions complete, you can begin shaping the sections of your paper—the paragraphs and the introduction and conclusion—to reflect your carefully considered goals.

Paragraphs

When you wrote a first draft, you probably considered the general principles of paragraphing, using each paragraph to develop what you thought to be one idea. It is difficult, however, to produce perfect paragraphs at the draft stage, especially if you are trying to write quickly. All too often, stray sentences will enter into your prose—and stay there—unless you revise carefully once you have finished drafting.

What you want, ultimately, is a series of paragraphs, all of which develop one particular idea clearly. Your first step in revision at this level involves what is called "glossing," determining the single idea being developed in each paragraph. To do this, read each paragraph. Try to sum up, in a sentence or less, what the central idea of the paragraph is. Then, read the paragraph over again. Are there any sentences which do not relate to this main point? Quite often, there will be. These should be eliminated, either by deleting them, placing them in another paragraph where they do fit, or reworking them so that their relevance to the controlling idea is made more clear. You may discover that your paragraph has two controlling ideas; in that case, produce two separate paragraphs, each with a controlling idea.

Once you have identified the main idea of each paragraph, you must ensure that it has been developed properly. Controlling ideas, like thesis statements, are assertions. As such they are not self-evident and need support. For this reason, as we have said before, a paragraph is rarely less than one hundred words. If your paragraphs are too short, ask yourself if you have developed the idea adequately. Perhaps you are presenting isolated points as paragraphs. If your paragraphs are too long (more than a page), you may be generalizing too much, or simply stringing ideas together. Look for ways of separating ideas or of breaking the main idea of long paragraphs into several component parts that could be developed in smaller paragraphs. Another possibility is that you might have been overzealous in your provision of evidence. Enough is enough.

Each paragraph must also read as a unified whole, advancing the main idea without losing the reader. There should be no difficulty in understanding how one sentence relates to another. Some tips on how to achieve unity follow.

1. *Pronouns.* You can use pronouns to maintain coherence while avoiding repetition. When you use a pronoun, make sure that it is obvious which noun it represents. A pronoun stands in pro—"on behalf of"—a particular noun, not a group of words or a whole

sentence. Avoid using "it" or "this" to refer to a sentence or idea. Vague pronoun reference is one of the principal sources of confusion in student essays.[6]

2. *Repetition.* It is not wrong to repeat a word several times in the same paragraph. In fact, repeating key words can tie sentences together clearly. However, if you suspect that hearing the word "liberalism" again would bore the reader, you can use a synonym or summary word to avoid repetition, and still sustain coherence by preceding it with a demonstrative adjective: hence "this political philosophy" or "that movement emphasizing liberty." If you use synonyms, be sure that they are exact, not thesaurus-style alternates. Do not substitute "power" for "authority" or "rights" for "privileges" merely to break the monotony. Note that this paragraph contains the words "repeat," "repeating," and "repetition": retaining the root word but modifying its grammatical form is another way of avoiding monotony without losing clarity.

3. *Transitional Words and Phrases.* These words and phrases can join ideas together in a sentence, sentences together in a paragraph, and paragraphs together in an essay. They are words like "equally," "subsequently," and "conversely"; phrases like "as a result," "for example," and "in conclusion." Even this incidental list shows how useful transitions are in unifying paragraphs. By linking ideas and, more importantly, by signalling the logical relation between the ideas they link, transitions indicate the main point of a paragraph and reveal how subordinate points relate to it. See "Appendix B: Transitional Words and Phrases" for a list of transitions grouped according to the logical relation they signify.

Exercise Three: Paragraph Structure and the Controlling Idea

Read the paragraphs below. Find the controlling idea of each paragraph, name the methods of organization used in each, and show how each is given coherence.

1. There are three groups which have caused the weakening of the Shah's position. First there are the mullahs, religious leaders who have lost not only land but also spiritual and secular influence during

---

[6]See page 152 for a further discussion of pronoun reference.

the Shah's reign. Second there are the Western-educated businessmen, professionals, and intellectuals, who are outraged by the Shah's denial of civil and political liberties and disappointed in his economic programmes. Then there are the students, whose concerns are diverse. Some side with the mullahs. Others side with the middle class in their dissatisfaction over economic progress. Still others are dedicated to establishing the outlawed Marxist Party.

2. In Placentia Bay, Newfoundland, fish have been found floating on the surface of the sea, red with the phosphorous lost from a chemical plant. In Lac Dufault, Québec, researchers have found high levels of copper, lead, zinc, cadmium, arsenic, and mercury from mining operations. In Pinchi Lake, British Columbia, there are no fish at all as a result of mercury pollution. Industrial wastes are upsetting nature's balance in every region of this country.

3. Beneath the epidermis lies a much thicker portion of the skin – the dermis. This consists basically of connective tissue, a type of material that is found throughout the body, filling in the interstices between the other structures. Here it is essentially a tough, felt-like material made up largely of a multitude of interlacing fibres. This tissue constitutes the greater amount of the thickness of the skin; prepared animal hide, such as the leather of our shoes, is entirely connective tissue.

4. During the five years following the passage of the Potlatch Law in 1884, no arrests were made. Then in August, 1889, a man was arrested and convicted of holding a potlatch. Three weeks later, however, the case was appealed and the prisoner discharged. In making his judgement, the Supreme Court Justice who heard the appeal questioned whether the law could be enforced at all because it did not adequately define "potlatch." The problem which he raised was only one of the problems which made the Potlatch Law difficult to enforce until it was omitted from the legislation in 1951.

Exercise Four: Paragraph Structure and Transitions within Paragraphs

Combine the following sentences into a paragraph. Make any little changes necessary such as inserting different transitional words to make the arrangement smooth. Note how the impact of the paragraph changes

130

as the arrangement improves, even though the ideas and evidence are the same.

> In the final section, as one might hope, Eliot talks about the rain that could bring relief to this waste land.

> The hope offered seems hard to accept, in contrast to the hard reality of the image of the waste land.

> The poem presents fragmented scenes of a purposeless, empty existence with no hope of renewal or resurrection.

> The image is one of hopeless desolation and spiritual dryness.

> It is too obscure, too disjointed.

> The poem ends in a storm of broken images that reflect the whole poem, but fail to give a clear way out of the problems it presents.

> The unravelling of a single image proves to be the key to all the others, for the images are intermeshed to the extent that, upon closer examination, the poem resolves itself into one image.

> Upon a rapid preliminary reading, *The Waste Land* appears to have no meaning at all.

> It is the image of the title – the waste land.

> The Hindu thunder proverb that he offers is alien enough to a Western reader that this resurrection seems almost forced or artificial.

Exercise Five: Paragraph Structure and Transitions within Paragraphs

Examine the introductory paragraph of the lobbying essay. How could the transitions between ideas be improved?

Incorporating Quotations in Paragraphs

As you know, if quotations are to be effective in your writing, they must be carefully worked into your own sentences and paragraphs. Sometimes at the draft stage it is difficult to think quickly about how a quotation might be positioned within your own prose. Since the tendency when we draft a paper is simply to plop quotations down where they seem useful, revising to ensure that quotations are introduced, commented on, and related to the controlling ideas of the paragraphs in which we have placed them is usually necessary. Also, the grace and argument of a sentence or a paragraph containing quotations should not be interrupted.

The note below is a direct quotation from Annette Tromly's *The Cover of the Mask: The Autobiographers in Charlotte Brontë's Fiction*. It is presented in the form of an offset quotation: indented on both sides, single-spaced, with no quotation marks. Following this presentation are several examples illustrating how part of this passage may be incorporated into a writer's own sentences.

> Jane's most important relationship exists in that strange imaginative mid-region half-way between illusion and reality. The genesis of the relationship goes as far back as Gateshead. Enclosed in the Red Room, Jane is torn by opposition and dominated by her literary imagination.[7]

1. Tromly argues that "Jane's most important relationship exists in that strange imaginative mid-region half-way between illusion and reality."

2. According to Tromly, "Jane's most important relationship exists in that strange imaginative mid-region half-way between illusion and reality."

3. "Jane's most important relationship" occurs, in Tromly's view, "half-way between illusion and reality."

These examples simply report Tromly's ideas, but they do so smoothly, and without abandoning the reader. The next two make a direct comment on the material quoted:

4. Tromly is wrong when she argues that "Jane's most important relationship exists in that strange imaginative mid-region half-way between illusion and reality."

5. Tromly argues convincingly that Jane Eyre's attachment to Rochester "exists in that strange imaginative mid-region half-way between illusion and reality."

---

[7] Annette Tromly, *The Cover of the Mask: The Autobiographers in Charlotte Brontë's Fiction*, English Literary Studies 26 (Victoria, B.C.: U of Victoria P) 53.

The last example places Tromly's ideas in context by referring to other researchers' treatment of the same topic:

6. All Brontë scholars agree with Tromly on one point: "Jane's most important relationship exists in that strange imaginative mid-region half-way between illusion and reality."

There are many ways to introduce quotations. When you see that you have repeated "X says" for the umpteenth time, consider an alternative from the following list:

according to
in the opinion of
as X adds, admits, affirms, argues,
    believes, confirms, declares,
    insists, mentions, proposes, reports,
    reveals, states, suggests, thinks,
    verifies

Exercise 6: Incorporating Quotations in Paragraphs

Examine how quotations are used in the following paragraphs taken from student essays. Do these quotations enhance a reader's understanding of each paragraph's controlling idea? Are all quotations introduced and commented on sufficiently? Decide which examples use quotations most effectively and gracefully, and which do not. Defend your decisions.

1. As in the past, Wilkes did not hesitate to capitalize on the popular support he had. But his motives remained consistently selfish as his own words attest.

    'I owe money in France, am an outlaw in
    England, hated by the King, the
    Parliament, and the bench of bishops...I
    must raise a dust or starve in a gaol; ...'[1]

Implicit in these words is an outright admission that if there had not been a danger of ending up in prison, Wilkes would not have put himself in front of the cause of liberty.

2. Not surprisingly, the wide number of bases on which a nation can be founded often leads to a variety of conceptions of the nation in any specific case. Africa serves as an excellent illustration of this. Minogue refers to pan-Africanism as "an imprecise aspiration based

on geography and colour."[2] On the other hand, the nation of Nigeria found itself confronted with the Biafran separatist movement.

3. Overwhelmed by the apparent change in Hamlet after he has assumed his "antic disposition," Ophelia cries:

> O! what a noble mind is here o'erthrown:
> The courtier's, soldier's, scholar's, eye,
> tongue, sword; (3.1.158-59)

It is clear that Goethe missed the total Hamlet and by this failure his understanding of the play was substantially limited. He saw only the gentleman and scholar of which Ophelia speaks but disregarded the equally significant "soldier" whose "sword" completed the line.

4. If these were the only references to war in the play then we might have a difficult time defending Hamlet as a man of strength. But he himself makes several allusions to battle strategy and fencing, an indication of his familiarity in such matters.

> For 'tis the sport to have the enginer
> Hoist with his own petar: and it shall go hard
> But I will delve one yard below their mines
> And blow them at the moon.... (3.4.206-09)

In direct reference to the ensuing conflict between himself and Claudius, Hamlet remarks on "the pass and fell incensed points / Of mighty opposites" (5.2.61-2).

Transitions Between Paragraphs

While it is important to revise the structure and contents of paragraphs so that they exhibit unity, it is equally important at the revision stage to make sure that each paragraph connects to the one preceding it and to the overall thesis of the paper. Writers can make use of the following transitional strategies to ensure that connections are clear for the reader.

1. Connect the preceding paragraph with the new one by reminding the reader of your thesis as you begin the paragraph.

Example: Clearly, then, our obstetrical procedures have not kept pace with our knowledge of infant psychology. Especially serious has been the early separation of the new-born from its mother.

2. Use a key word from the preceding paragraph.

   Example: Our increased attention to psychological tendencies such as bonding [discussed in previous paragraph] should lead to new hospital procedures.

3. Use a transitional word or phrase. (See the previous explanation and the list of transitions in Appendix B.)

4. Begin the paragraph with a sentence that glances backward to the last paragraph and forward to the new one.

   Example: If the last decade has witnessed many changes in theory [subject of preceding paragraph], practice has not kept pace.

Exercise Seven: Transitions Between Paragraphs

Look for the transitional devices used by the writer of the essay on lobby groups to begin new paragraphs. How could you make use of the techniques described above to improve the links between paragraphs?

Introductions

There are other, special kinds of sections that demand attention at the revision stage. One such section is the group of paragraphs which constitute your essay's introduction. This section will almost invariably need to be revised, since it is likely that when you first drafted it you really didn't know what you were introducing. Also, be assured that most of us lack confidence when we begin to write. The experience of fumbling and straining and going off course frustrates and upsets us. That is why we advised writing the first draft of your introduction with no other aim than to find your bearings. A complete revision, consequently, is necessary because much of what you have written will be long-winded ruminations, wordy circlings about, and other manners of false starts. Now is the time to consider capturing your reader's attention with a revised introduction that is both eloquent and witty.

How should you revise your introduction? What should it do? It is only fair that your introduction provide the reader with information which accurately foreshadows the general nature of the essay: you, after all, expect to be able to predict the content of other people's work when you skim their introductory paragraphs. An introduction should genuinely "introduce" what you have to say, "lead" the essay "into" your readers' minds in such a way that they will not feel misinformed once the essay gets underway. Your statement of purpose or thesis may appear in the introductory paragraph, but it alone will not make a good introduction to your essay. Also, your introduction should not reproduce the bluntness of your outline in paragraph form. Be more than merely accurate: try to show your readers something interesting enough or attractive enough about your essay so that they will anticipate reading it with some pleasure. Following are some suggestions that may help you to revise your introductions:

1. Provide some background information before stating the thesis. This information should not necessarily be used to advance the thesis but should provide an interesting context for it.

2. Raise a question (or series of questions) which your essay will consider, and save the answer for the conclusion. A question may attract the reader more quickly than a declaration. Using a question is not, however, permission to sit on the fence, wander, or otherwise neglect your thesis.

3. State the problem or dilemma which your essay will resolve and the circumstances that led to its emergence. You might summarize the solutions to be considered in your essay.

4. Emphasize the difference between your evidence and that of other researchers, or between your interpretation and someone else's. Such an introduction places your essay in the context of scholarly debate.

5. Use a quotation from either a primary or secondary source. You might choose a passage that captures the main focus of your work. Controversial quotations can kindle the reader's imagination, and ones that you disagree with and disprove can make sparks fly.

6. Anticipate the reader's possible objections to your approach or interpretation and show quickly why they are not valid.

7. Begin with a paradox or apparent contradiction.

8. Begin with a specific example, illustration, or anecdote that is interesting and apt.

9. Define the scope of your investigation. Indicate its parameters and your reasons for choosing them.

10. If you are writing in a discipline such as philosophy or sociology, you may wish to define clearly the way in which you will use particular words, or the way in which you interpret certain words used in the work you are writing about.

Avoid:

1. "The purpose of this essay is to prove that...." In fact, avoid all conspicuously self-conscious announcements of what you have done, are doing, or will do. Usually the sentence survives excision of such nervous words, and is the stronger for it. If the sentence collapses, it did not contain an assertion and needs to be rewritten. Instead of saying, "First I will examine the east and then the west, and finally relate the two together," say "While it normally rises in the east, the morning sun has been sighted in the west by cattle ranchers in Alberta, and can be shown at times to appear in both horizons simultaneously."

2. Dictionary definitions. These are boring, and rarely help.

3. The opening sentence which echoes the instructor's question or the essay title, or depends upon the title to be understood. Such a sentence indicates a lack of understanding and imagination. Especially do not say, "I will now answer Question Number 3." Anyone, not just the instructor, should be able to understand your introduction.

4. The inflated declaration of a cliché or a commonplace idea. For example, "Ever since the dawn of mankind people have needed to eat/ engaged in war/ searched for meaning/ loved the simple pleasures."

5. Apologizing for your subject or opinions. Nervous noises such as "In the limited time and space of a term paper...," "As a novice in the discipline...," and so on, should be edited out. If you are feeling nervous, tell your dog. Do not tell your instructor, at least not in your essay.

6. Gratuitous personal preambles. "At first I thought biology was dull but then I had a great teacher in grade 12 and after doing the research for this essay I really think I might major in it...." You are tempting your instructor to respond, "Who cares?"

Exercise Eight: Introductions

Decide which of the following are good introductory paragraphs, and try to name the method of introduction used.

1. (From an essay on John Wilkes)
   In 1763, at the approximate mid-point in his life, John Wilkes joined the cause of liberty. It was an alliance that was to prove beneficial to Wilkes as well as to the cause of which he made himself the symbol. The events from 1763 into the 1770s are ironic in the extreme: a man whose main, perhaps only, motivation was self-interest had the effect of furthering the interests of all men.

2. (From an essay on the Prometheus myth)
   This is an attempt to discuss the Prometheus myth with the aid of pictures and quotations from ancient authors. Sophocles called him "The Lord of Fire." Aeschylus sees Prometheus in the role of fire bringer, as evidenced by the title *Prometheus The Fire Bringer,* one of two lost plays in the Promethean trilogy.

3. (From an essay on Frank Lloyd Wright and Louis Sullivan)
   Louis Sullivan and Frank Lloyd Wright, two important American architects who began to claim the attention of the international architectural community in the late 1800s, both advocated the tenets of "functionalism," the most important architectural movement of the early twentieth century. Because they were contemporaries and both proponents of functionalism, Sullivan and Wright are often looked upon as having made similar contributions to architecture. However, the buildings they designed demonstrate their differing interpretations of the new architectural concept.

4. (From an essay on fantasy and reality in *Who's Afraid of Virginia Woolf?)*
   Richard Schechner, editor of the *Tulane Drama Review,* greeted Edward Albee's *Who's Afraid of Virginia Woolf?* with the charge that it was "a persistent escape into morbid fantasy."[3] But does the play really urge us "to escape reality," as Mr. Schechner maintains?[4] Although the play is certainly concerned with fantasy and reality, fantasy is hardly shown as the more desirable alternative. Indeed, in the final moments of the drama, the characters are brought to a head-on confrontation with reality.

5. (From an essay on utopian and scientific socialists)
This essay will deal with history. At first, this seems to be a ridiculous statement for a history term paper, but everything that appears to be is not always so.

6. (From an essay on the Progressive movement)
The Progressive movement represents a radical departure from traditional Canadian politics. The first federal "third party" elected to Parliament, it channelled western agrarian discontent toward Ottawa and made eastern politicians aware of the prairie voice in Canadian politics.

7. (From an essay on *Wuthering Heights*)
One of the best novels in literature is the novel *Wuthering Heights*. Early in the nineteenth century author Emily Brontë wrote this brilliant plot. But, as the world turns, so do the critics. One in particular, James Hafley, argues that Nelly Dean is a villain. In my essay I hope to refute Hafley's views.

8. (From an essay on the CCF)
The CCF party in Canada had elements in common with the Labour party in Britain, another socialist party. Socialism is a very broad term, and it encompasses many different ideologies and strategies. In fact, the CCF party was quite different from the NDP party which grew out of it. And of course there are differences between national and regional organizations in the NDP.

9. (From an essay on school closure)
Declining enrolment in recent years has left many schools half empty, and economic hard times have put school trustees under pressure from taxpayers to reduce the high costs of education. However, the obvious solution—to close schools—is often met with furious protests by parents and neighbourhood groups. Does the closing of schools have the harsh economic and social effects on the community that parents fear? And if so, are there viable alternatives to the problems caused by fewer students and a shrinking dollar?

10. (From an essay on treason)
Why do people commit treason? By looking at four British spies, Burgess, Maclean, Philby, and Blount, who were recruited for the Soviet Union in the 1930s, I will try to understand why a man might spy against his country. However, I am neither a spy nor British,

and so it is possible that I might not really understand the psychology of the spy.

Conclusions

However difficult it is to write and revise an introduction, drawing a piece of prose to an effective conclusion is even more challenging. The chief block to producing a good conclusion is coming to the hard realization that endings are exclusive not inclusive, that in finishing something we are never pretending to have exhausted the topic. An essay, like a life, may be concluded but it can never be complete: there will always be something left undone. Once we acknowledge this fact, the anxiety over the completion of a work can be converted into the pleasure of rhetorical closure, of saying good-bye to the reader in an informative and witty manner. Finishing an essay is not unlike leaving a room or departing a party: You want your audience to remember you and to think and speak well of you when you are gone.

The effective conclusion to an essay stimulates the reader to think more about the topic, and to think about it in a critically open-minded way. While it should return the reader to the larger view of the terrain you have covered, a conclusion should not just reiterate the premise and method set out in the introduction. To "say what you are going to do" in the introduction, to "do it" in the body of the paper, and to "point out that you've done it" in the conclusion is not to write an essay. In fact, a conclusion may well posit a new beginning by suggesting further avenues of pursuit which could not be dealt with because of the formal limitations of the writing.

Although the best conclusions are creative, they also exude a sense of the writer's control. One should "feel" the essay coming to a close, just as one would feel a piece of music resolving the variations upon its theme into one last expression; in this sense, a conclusion is as much a matter of tone as of content, less what one says than how one says it. Following are some suggestions on how to say it:

1. In an essay that has begun with a question, include the answer in the conclusion.

2. Use a significant quotation (probably not from a secondary source) that supports the thesis.

3. Use an anecdote that supports the thesis.

4. If your essay has pointed out a problem or a number of problems,

use the last paragraph to suggest solutions. These problems do not have to be solved completely. Complex problems rarely are.

5. Widen the perspective in the concluding paragraph: show how your thesis has implications beyond the immediate scope of the essay. Be careful, however, not to jump tracks into a whole new topic, or to introduce ideas that you ought to have considered in the essay.

Avoid:

1. "In conclusion (or in summary) I have proved that...." The reader's natural response will be "Oh, have you?"

2. Minor details or afterthoughts. Do not be anti-climactic. If you cannot bear to throw out the gems that you could not fit smoothly into the essay, consider using them as supplementary notes.

3. Qualifying remarks.

4. Apologizing for your opinions.

5. Obvious expressions, fan-mail about literature, writers, historical characters. It is admirable to reveal excellence where it exists, but not to rave about it adoringly instead of relating it usefully to your thesis.

While your conclusion should not echo your introduction, presenting the two as a pair can be effective if, in concluding, you go beyond what you have said in the introduction. You might look for a pair of quotations, or anecdotes, or events, for example, that seem to capture the essence of the way you see the topic. Symmetry provides a satisfying sense of having come full circle, the journey done, and (assuming you have shown the reader something along the way) of having advanced in insight and understanding.

However you decide to end, do not apologize for your inadequacies. In the words of Nellie McClung, early twentieth-century feminist reformer and member of the Alberta legislature, "Never retreat, never explain, never apologize. Get the thing done and let them howl."[8]

---

[8] Nellie McClung, quoted in *New Canadian Quotations*, ed. John Robert Columbo (Edmonton: Hurtig, 1987) 2b.

Exercise Nine: Conclusions

Decide which of the following would make good concluding paragraphs, and try to name the method of conclusion used.

1. (From an essay on the Progressive movement)
   In conclusion, I believe that I have proven that the Progressive movement conveyed western agrarian discontent to Ottawa and made politicians in the east aware of prairie concerns.

2. (From an essay on the use of corporal punishment in schools)
   "Spare the rod and spoil the child": no enlightened educator these days believes in that old adage. The research we have looked at shows clearly that corporal punishment in schools not only arouses great resentment in the child toward school and authority figures but also unwittingly teaches that problems can be solved by the use of physical force. And yet many teachers are loathe to ban the strap. What measures could be introduced that would alleviate teachers' fears that the banning of corporal punishment would bring anarchy to the classroom? Administrators could perhaps reduce teachers' anxieties by providing smaller classes so that teachers could give more individual attention to each child; by seeing that teachers are aware of the newer teaching techniques which minimize confrontation; and by making sure that troubled children are seen quickly by guidance counsellors or outside agencies before their problems become acute.

3. (From an essay on John Wilkes)
   Wilkes did not suffer from his alliance with Liberty. Engraved on his coffin are the words,

   > The remains of John Wilkes,
   > a Friend of Liberty.[5]

   Not "Crusader," nor "Champion" simply "Friend." This is a fitting phrase for a man who well knew what a useful friend the cause of Liberty could be.

4. (From an essay on research into cancer)
   Scientists, then, believe that a cure for cancer will come not from goal-oriented research but from basic research into areas not directly related to cancer. Incidentally, much modern knowledge has arisen from basic research, the implications of which the researcher was never aware. Newton invented calculus so that he could mathematically explain the motion of the heavenly bodies. He had

no idea that his invention would enable man to plot the journey of a spaceship to the moon.

5. (From an essay on techniques of characterization in Tolstoy's *War and Peace*)

   Tolstoy's *War and Peace* is a very long novel with a great many characters. If Tolstoy had not been able to make the characters stand out from each other and seem real, this book would have been difficult to follow. As it was, the novel was a pleasure to read.

6. (From an essay on chemical pollution in the Walney River)

   The effects of the disposal of chemical waste into the Walney River at Barrow are alarming. But Barrow is only a small town of 6,000, with only one large industrial operation. Add to this picture the pollutants that are pouring into rivers from major cities which are a hundred, two hundred, even three hundred times as large as Barrow, and the size and complexity of the regional problems become apparent.

7. (From an essay on the fall of Berlin)

   Of course the conclusions I have reached may not be the only conclusions possible. Those who were there fighting, reporting, directing may have understood the fall of Berlin differently. History will never know who is right.

8. (From an essay on the problems of closing schools)

   Closing a school that has strong ties with the community it serves can have deleterious economic and social effects on the whole community. To avoid such harmful results, many school boards have managed to keep schools open and yet balance their budgets by trimming all unnecessary expenditures. Most notably, they have cut administrative costs, and they have provided innovative programmes which attract particular groups of students (such as adult and foreign students) who would not otherwise attend the school. Trustees should consider their options very carefully before they walk the political tightrope of closing schools.

9. (From an essay on Einstein's place in modern physics)

   When Einstein was asked by a reporter why he did not take along a notebook on his afternoon walks so that he could jot down any important ideas he might have, Einstein replied: "Well, you see, I have so few important ideas."[6] Humility was as vital a part of his genius as was the intuition which led him to see which ideas were truly great. Einstein gave to modern physics three very great ideas, and of few scientists can as much be said.

10. (From an essay on Canadian and American relations in the early 1960s)

The poor relationship between the Diefenbaker and Kennedy governments of the early 1960s was, as we have seen, caused by complicated political and historical factors. It has just occurred to me that the characters and backgrounds of Mr. Diefenbaker and Mr. Kennedy—one a Baptist, the other a Catholic, one from a modest, the other from a rich and influential background—might have had as much to do with the misunderstandings between the governments as any political cause.

Exercise Ten: Introductions and Conclusions

Three of the introductory and concluding paragraphs in the previous exercises correspond to each other. Find the pairs and comment on how well or poorly they work together.

Exercise Eleven: Introductions and Conclusions

Read the introductory and concluding paragraphs of the three sample essays. What are the strengths and weaknesses of these paragraphs? Consider these introductions and conclusions in relation to the content of the essay. How could they be improved?

Checklist: Revising Sections

Paragraphs

1. What is the controlling idea of each of your paragraphs?

2. Have you developed these ideas sufficiently?

3. How long are your paragraphs? Are they shorter than three sentences or do they cover two pages?

4. Are there gaps between the ideas expressed at the end of one paragraph and those expressed at the beginning of the one following it?

5. Have you signalled your reader as to the relations within and between paragraphs by using transitions?

6. Do all of the quotations used contribute to the meaning and unity of the paragraphs in which you have placed them? Is every quotation introduced and commented on sufficiently? Have you worked quotations into your prose gracefully?

Introductions and Conclusions

1. Does your introduction give a clear idea of what the essay is about?

2. How long is your introduction? Do you bore your readers with a wordy introduction, or do you fail to capture their interest because your introduction consists of a bald, unappealing statement of purpose or thesis?

3. Does your essay have a forceful, interesting, and obvious conclusion, or does it seem to wither away?

4. Is your conclusion merely a restatement of your introduction and a précis of your paper, or does it show growth?

5. Does your conclusion read more like the introduction to another essay?

Revising Sentences

Many revisions take place at the sentence level. When examining your first draft, consider how to order your words better, whether your words are well-chosen, and whether your sentences correspond to grammatical conventions. These three elements — syntax, diction, and grammar — work together to make your sentences coherent.

Revising Syntax

Syntax provides a sentence with a kind of neurological system. It communicates and coordinates the intention behind the expression of the sentence; it enacts and articulates the desires and objectives behind the thought of the writer. When this system breaks down, the sentence loses its balance, becoming uncoordinated, and the development of meaning is paralyzed. During revision, such dysfunctional sentences must be rehabilitated through the proper use of coordination, subordination, and parallel structure.

Coordination and Subordination

The seven coordinating conjunctions (and, but, or, for, nor, so, yet) are used to link ideas of equal value or to add those ideas together. Unfortunately, many students view the coordinating conjunctions as the sole means of linking ideas within sentences, the result being that clauses which were never intended to be equal are often made to appear so. To relate two ideas that are unequal in rank, a writer can employ subordination (from the Latin meaning "placed lower in rank"); the greater variety of relations possible is reflected in the dozens of conjunctions and relative pronouns used to subordinate. Conjunctions such as "when," "where," "because," and "although" illustrate and define the hierarchy of a sentence; they indicate how the subordinate ideas surround and support the principal concept in the sentence. They may introduce elements of time, cause, purpose, or condition—the when, how, why, and if of an idea. In the simplest sense, subordination compels otherwise isolated ideas to interact and thereby reveal their dominant or submissive positions in the sentence. Consider this example:

1. He cooks. She eats.
2. When he cooks, she eats.
3. Because he cooks, she eats.
4. He cooks so that she can eat.
5. Although he cooks, she eats.

In the first instance we know nothing about the relationship between he and she, and we can merely assume that she is eating what he cooks. Subordination not only immediately relates the two acts but, in the two subsequent examples, gives us respectively a simple temporal or causal basis for the relation of the cooking to the eating. Examples 3, 4, and 5 each begin through subordination to intimate something about the motives and dynamics that connect he to she as individual personalities. And in example 5, the simple use of "although" suggests a possible injustice or inadequacy in the relationship between these two people: does she eat and get all the advantages of nutrition even though it is he who cooks and does all the preparation? Or, does she eat out of sheer politeness or graciousness even though his cooking is not especially good? Through such implications the sentence has become dynamic: its static observations have been transformed into elements that are related.

Exercise Twelve: Revising Syntax through Coordination and Subordination

Combine the following sentences using coordinating and subordinating conjunctions as well as relative pronouns. There is a list of these words in Appendix C. Think about the complex sentences you create. Which of these sentences express interesting ideas worthy of further investigation? Write the paragraphs suggested by these sentences.

1. Nuclear power is costly.
   Nuclear power produces potentially deadly wastes.
   We do not yet know how to dispose of these wastes safely.

2. North American Indians suffered from sicknesses.
   They recognized these sicknesses as European.
   They would often accept European remedies.

3. I saw a wild hog foraging in the woods.
   The hog's face was covered with mud.
   It reminded me of my brother eating spaghetti.

4. Car manufacturers spend millions of dollars on research.
   They spend this money to develop small horsepower engines.
   These engines will travel twice as far on a gallon of gas as today's engines.

5. Scientists must be aware of the advantages of their discoveries.
   They must be equally aware of the disadvantages of their discoveries.
   Their role is difficult.

Parallel Structure

Parallel structure treats two elements of a sentence as equal in rank. The structure is used to list elements or to compare them, and because of the grammatical similarity of the elements, the reader is able to hold them together in mind. Parallelism thus encourages the connecting, building, integrating activity of mind that makes for exciting reading. It enhances writing in the way that analogy does: an effective parallelism will make the reader feel an active part of the intellectual movement of a sentence. All this is due to the symmetrical repetition of phrases and grammatical constructions within parallel units of a sentence. Consider the following example:

> In our primitive past, survival was a physical struggle against
> famine, war, and pestilence; in our contemporary world, it is

an intellectual struggle against apathy, selfishness, and
isolation.

Here the structure itself is relatively simple, but the activity of mind it
sets up is rich and complex. The parallel structure begins with an
opposition of past and present predicates ("was" and "is") across the
fulcrum of the semi-colon. The tension extends to semantic contrasts:
"primitive" and "contemporary" times, "physical" and "intellectual" struggles. The meaning, however, resides in the association of psychological
conditions like "apathy, selfishness, and isolation" with the historic evils
of "famine, war, and pestilence." What is a group concern in the first
half of the sentence is applied to the individual in the second to evoke
an inescapably critical and pessimistic conclusion; the ultimate import
of the sentence is thus more implied than stated.

Exercise Thirteen: Revising Syntax by Employing Parallel Structure

Write sentences that parallel those below in structure and in general
intent. Use punctuation to relate the sentence you have created to the
one given, and see what the resultant sentences imply.

1. Our purpose should be to discover the truth rather than to prove
   ourselves right.

2. We judge our friends by their words and by their deeds.

3. Punctuation is analogous to musical notation in its function.

4. We have no right to consume happiness without producing it.

5. One's will reigns at twenty years of age.

Revising Diction

Diction refers both to a writer's choice of words and to the art of speaking
itself. It is useful to remember this dual definition since good writing
is close to good spoken English, that is, to English as it is seldom spoken.
Your words should invite understanding rather than repel it; they should
be natural enough to say aloud without seeming awkward or pretentious.
Sentences should not appear to have resulted from a laborious effort to
construct a marvel of linguistic engineering through heavy reliance on
dictionaries or thesauri. Neither should they be chatty or slangish,
because such language is not precise enough to declare rigorous thought.
At times, academic writers need polysyllabic words and complex syntax;

a thesis adequately argued entirely in short sentences of five-letter words is probably simplistic and bitty (with apologies to Ernest Hemingway). But understanding writing is difficult enough without allowing language to complicate what it is intended to declare. Readers who have to struggle through difficult diction to excavate the meaning of a sentence are not happy when they find it rattling around like a pea in a drum. When you revise your diction, try to think of getting the right fit between your thought and your words.

Also, try to eliminate redundant words from your first draft. Do not, however, slash too many words. Your sentences should have a rhythmic, flowing quality, and if you carve them down to their bare bones they will read in a choppy, staccato fashion. Worse still, they might not communicate your exact meaning. Be neither lavish nor stingy with your language: use as many words as you need and no more.

Since the twin purposes of writing are to refine and to communicate thought, we should try to choose words accurately. Our words should exactly convey our thoughts. Easy advice to give, but difficult to follow. Every individual's understanding of words is different; you and I will probably picture two distinct people when we read the word "extremist." To me, an extremist could be a male banker who doesn't wear a suit and tie to work. You might think any banker or anyone who works extreme. Because of the possibility that they will be misunderstood, writers must revise to eliminate vague words. Keep in mind that general, abstract words, while necessary in essay writing, can be misinterpreted by your reader more readily than specific, concrete words. Upon reading "athlete" you might think of a hockey player, I might think of a rower, and the next person might think of a cyclist. However, we would probably all think of a Canadian sprinter if we read "Ben Johnson" instead.

Another reason to use concrete words in essays is that they show rather than tell your reader what you mean. Poets and novelists rarely rely on abstract words to convey meaning, yet the concrete words they use often express general emotions or ideas. Philosophers, too, usually flush out their abstract theories with concrete examples. Often, these examples are more memorable than the universals they illuminate. We recall with ease Plato's discussion of a table while we forget his theory of forms. Remember, then, to revise your writing so that your diction is as specific, concrete, and precise as it can be.

Try also to choose words fairly. As we have seen, all words have con-notations as well as denotations. Although the words "agreement" and "deal" both mean or denote "an arrangement," the first has a favourable connotation while the second's connotation is unfavourable (an interesting thing to consider if you are reading or writing about free trade in Canada). Most writers use the connotative power of words to make their writing expressive and to give it texture, but words that slant your interpretation of truth should be avoided.

Exercise Fourteen: Revising Diction

Below are five versions of the same idea. These versions all use different sorts of words to communicate this idea. Identify the best passage, explain why you chose it, and tell why you didn't choose the other four.

1. Writing carefully is important. It conveys meaning to the reader. Clear writing helps us to think. Employers consider it important.

2. The written medium is oriented toward a dual goal. First, it must provide input for the user. Second, it must capitalize on the interface between thought and symbol.

3. Clear writing refines our thoughts and enables communication with our readers.

4. It is incumbent on the aspiring writer of serious prose to be cognizant of his responsibility to strive for the utmost clarity of elucidation. Since language is inextricably related to the cognitive faculties, we are capable of cultivating our thinking by rendering our language with ultimate precision.

5. It is important to get close to what you mean when you write. Otherwise, the person who's reading your writing won't understand it. Also, you won't be able to get your own ideas down on paper.

Exercise Fifteen: Revising Diction

Revise the following paragraph, or one that you have written, making each noun and verb as specific and concrete as possible. Note that this revision eliminates the fuzzy thinking that sneaks into writing when general words are used.

> Macbeth wanted power more than anything else. His wife wanted the same thing. So they were really both the same. She talked him into doing what they did, but really they both wanted

to. After they did it, they saw things and didn't talk to each other as much as they used to. Finally, everything came true and Macbeth was killed. Hamlet was the same as them, only he had to talk himself into doing it. King Lear was the same, only he didn't want power; he wanted power back. And *Othello* has always been a problem. Perhaps Francis Bacon wrote it.

Revising Grammar

Conventional grammar is not the creation of demonic composition teachers; followed carefully, it does help a reader understand your writing. Try to think of it as a series of signals to your reader, as a tool aiding communication rather than as an end in itself. Completing any number of drills or exercises designed to teach grammatical rules is useless if you don't learn to use grammar to express yourself in your own particular way. Therefore, always consider the meaning you want to convey before scurrying to a grammar text in search of a rule to assist in its conveyance.

Most students make only a few grammatical errors, but they make these same errors over and over again. It is difficult, however, to find a commonality of error. There are as many different grammatical mistakes made as there are individuals to make them. For this reason, and because of the limits of space, we will not provide you with a complete explanation of the conventions of grammar. Such a task is better left to grammar texts. We propose instead to assist you in the creation of your own checklist, one that will help you catch and revise the grammatical errors you frequently make. Initially, you should compile this checklist by considering the following points in light of a returned essay that has been thoroughly commented on and corrected by one of your instructors. Keep revising your personal checklist, however, for the sorts of grammatical errors you make will change as your knowledge of grammatical conventions expands.

1. *Has your instructor inserted commas in your text?* If the answer is yes, try to discern where you generally forget to use commas. Perhaps you neglect to place them after introductory words, phrases, or clauses. The sentences "However she looks to the stars for inspiration" and "Built on the site of Byzantium Constantinople became the capital of the Roman Empire" are desperately in need of commas after their introductory elements. Commas also may be used, however, to surround a phrase or word that interrupts the flow of your sentence.

In the sentence above, "however" is enclosed by commas because it is interjectory. In such cases, it may be easier to decide whether to use commas by reading your sentences aloud to see where pauses make sense than by learning the grammatical rules about restrictive clauses, non-restrictive clauses, and interjections that govern their use. Remember to insert commas only where you pause in speech, not where you pause in thought. Do you forget to use commas when listing things? Your sentences should contain commas which separate words, phrases, or clauses listed in a series – as this sentence does.

2. *Do you ever use semi-colons and colons?* These punctuation marks are often neglected even though they are invaluable in associating two or more ideas. As we have seen, a semi-colon can communicate complicated meanings when used to form a parallel structure. A colon can effectively introduce what follows it: a single word, a list of words, an independent clause, or a quotation.

3. *Do you tend to omit or misplace apostrophes that indicate possession?* Most students understand that they should write "a dog's breakfast," "Cohen's poem," "women's rights," and "ten cents' worth," but they are frequently confused about how to form the possessive of a tiny word: it. Remembering that "it's" means "it is" and that there is no such word as "its' " will help you write "its" when you mean "its importance" or "its beauty."

4. *Has your instructor circled or crossed out exclamation points or question marks?* Exclamation points are only supposed to follow truly emphatic, exclamatory sentences like "The President has pressed the button!" Since these exclamations do not frequent scholarly prose, exclamation points should rarely appear in your essays. Question marks are used to indicate direct questions. "He asked if the ozone layer would disappear altogether" is an indirect question, a statement really, so it would end with a period. "Will you please stop smoking" is a polite request which should also close with a period.

5. *Has your instructor indicated that sometimes the grammatical units of your sentences do not agree with one another?* Subjects and verbs should agree in number. Most people do this routinely, but sometimes there is an occasional slip if a sentence's verb is far away from its subject. For example, a writer might have had difficulty making the subject and verb agree in the following grammatically

152

correct sentence. "The Prime Minister, along with many other politicians, civil servants, and government appointees, opposes this initiative." A pronoun must also agree in number with the noun it refers to; it must be plural if its antecedent is plural, and singular if its antecedent is singular. "Typical students, while concerned about grades, essay deadlines, and imminent exams, have time to explore some of the athletic, social, cultural, and intellectual benefits open to them at university." In this sentence, the antecedent "students" is plural as is the pronoun "them."

6. *Are your pronoun references clear?* If a pronoun's antecedent is remote, ambiguous, vague, or missing, readers will be confused.

a) *Remote Reference.* Pronouns that are distant from the nouns they refer to often cause readers to search through prose for meaning. In the following passage, the pronoun "it" is too remote from its antecedent "meningitis."

> Meningitis is an inflammation of the tissue covering the brain and spinal cord. Symptoms include headaches, vomiting, and fever. Sufferers also complain that light hurts their eyes, that they cannot bend their necks without pain, and that they are drowsy. Anyone with these symptoms should see a doctor as it is an uncommon but serious condition.

b) *Ambiguous Reference.* If a pronoun might refer to more than one noun, its reference is ambiguous. In the sentence "We admired Jane's prize-winning Newfoundland bitch while she went off to find her offspring," the pronouns "she" and "her" could refer either to Jane or to the bitch.

c) *Vague Reference.* Misuse of the pronoun "this" is most likely to cause this error: "Donovan's argument that the American political system dilutes pressures in American society for more economic equality is well-founded. This is complicated by the political power of wealthy interest groups." Here, the writer could be referring either to Donovan's argument or to the process whereby pressure for economic equality is diluted.

d) *Missing Antecedent.* A pronoun must refer to a noun. If this noun is only implicit, is nowhere named, then the pronoun is said to be missing its antecedent. "As she watched the sailboat, it suddenly got up, filling the sails." Obviously, the writer means that the wind got up, not the sailboat.

7. *Has the relation between a modifying word or phrase and the element modified been made clear?* Misplaced modifiers can create vague or unintentionally humorous sentences: "The minister chatted informally about the cost of living with several women." Presumably, the minister is chatting informally with several women, not chatting about how much it costs to live with several women. Sometimes, a modifier squints, looking both to its left and to its right in search of a word or phrase to modify. In the sentence "Post offices are open on Saturdays only in the country," we don't know whether "only" modifies "on Saturdays" or "in the country." Occasionally, a modifier will dangle unattached to any word in the sentence that is its nominal home. Dangling modifiers are frequently verbal phrases within sentences written using the passive voice: "After lying, stealing, swearing, smoking, playing hooky, and winning a Sunday School prize by fraud, a small fortune in gold is Tom Sawyer's at the end of the story." The small fortune in gold does not lie, steal, swear, smoke, play hooky, or win prizes; Tom does.

8. *Do your sentences tend to be too exclusive or too inclusive; do you frequently create sentence fragments, fused sentences, or comma splices?* No matter how many times "A nice way to start saving for a Steinway" flashes on your television screen, it is still a sentence fragment because it does not contain a subject or a conjugated verb. You are most likely to write a sentence fragment that has both a subject and a verb but that is incomplete because it depends upon another clause for meaning. Neither "But only for charity, never for pay" nor "When I returned in the evening" are sentences. The first is a coordinate clause and the second is a subordinate clause. A fused sentence occurs when two sentences or independent clauses are run together without any punctuation between them: "The love of liberty is the love of others the love of power is the love of ourselves." A comma splice creates a similar jamming together of independent clauses even though these two clauses are separated by a comma: "Each dog grows to resemble its owner, that is its tragedy." Comma splices frequently occur because writers mistakenly believe that conjunctive adverbs such as "consequently," "however," "therefore," and "nevertheless" have the connecting power of conjunctions like "and" and "but." An example of this sort of comma splice follows: "Road repairs may cause traffic jams, nevertheless, some repairs must be made even during heavy traffic."

Exercise Sixteen: Revising Grammar

Write down the lyrics of a popular song that you consider meaningful. You have probably written them using the punctuation of poetry or no punctuation at all. Make this "poem" into properly punctuated prose.

Exercise Seventeen: Revising Grammar

The following paragraph contains examples of some common errors in grammar. There are nine in total. Read the passage aloud to help you identify them all. Then, revise the passage to correct its grammar and to make stylistic and syntactic improvements.

> To "sum" an existence, "bound" a life, and find safety in the "strait limits" of an enclosed mind.[4] This must of been the motive of the fictional autobiographers of Charlotte Brontë's novels. Because all three autobiographers seem to need to oversimplify both their own natures and the worlds in which they live in. They are all different, however, they go and do it in basically the same way! Repressing what her more instinctual impulses tell her about the complex truths of experience; this is how they generate personal mythologies by which to rationalize their lives.

Checklist: Revising Sentences

Syntax

1. Are the ideas expressed within each sentence properly linked through coordination or subordination? If you depend upon coordinate conjunctions inordinately, you might unintentionally be making unequal ideas appear equal.

2. Have you used parallel structure to connect and compare sentence elements and the thoughts they represent?

3. Are your sentences generally balanced and symmetrical?

Diction

1. Have you used language which is clear and easy to understand?

2. Are there any words which have not been adequately defined?

3. Have you avoided slang and jargon? Are the words you use too informal, or have you written in a kind of "bureaucratese" or "computerese"?

4. Is your language as concise as possible? Eliminate deadwood, redundancies, and trite expressions. Don't be self-indulgent. Cut unnecessary words and clever but irrelevant asides.

5. Is your language so sparse and simple that you risk boring your reader? Make sure you have enough words to express your meaning in an exciting way.

6. Have you always attempted to use an exact word to convey your precise meaning?

7. Do your words tend to be general or specific, abstract or concrete? You should usually choose the concrete word unless an abstract word is more accurate.

8. Have you used words fairly?

Grammar

1. Check to see if your grammar is conventional by using the personal checklist you have prepared.

Part Two: Proofreading

Proofreading is not the same as revising. While revising means looking again at the whole of your first draft and its constituent parts, proofreading implies taking a last look at your almost complete essay. Since "proof" is a publishing term for the typeset version of a writer's text, by the time a writer reads a proof, it is very close to its final version. Proofreading is the writer's last chance to check this text for minor errors before it is sent to the printing press.

Students, to proofread their essays effectively, should provide themselves with a fairly legible and accurate revised draft. After all, it will be difficult to catch spelling errors, faulty documentation, and inaccurate citations if the drafts they proof are sloppy.

A checklist of things to consider while proofreading follows. One last point before we get to it. The copy you submit to your instructor should be proofread with as much attention as your revised draft. If you type this copy, or have it typed, correct any typographical errors. Use pen and ink if you have to. While it is to your advantage to make the essay submitted as attractive and professional-looking as possible, it is better to catch and change mistakes than to give your instructor a neat but incorrect paper.

Checklist: Proofreading[9]

1. **Are your words spelled correctly?** Sometimes there are two or more ways to spell the same word. Ensure that you choose one variation and stick to it.

2. **When you have needed to divide words at the ends of lines, have you done so properly?** In such instances, a word should be divided at syllable breaks. Consult a dictionary if you cannot decipher where these breaks occur.

3. **Have you corrected typographical errors neatly?**

4. **How are numbers expressed in your text?** There are certain conventions to follow here. Usually, numbers that can be expressed in one or two words are written out. However, if the numbers are long, or if you are listing more than one number in a sentence, using numerals is preferable. Do not begin a sentence with a numeral in any circumstance.

5. **Have you indicated which words and phrases in your text are titles?** Quotation marks should be placed around the titles of chapters of books, articles, short stories, and short poems. The titles of other works, such as complete books, journals, plays, and films, should be either underlined or printed in italics.

6. **Have you used the proper form when quoting?**

7. **Do you cite all of your sources using a standard, acceptable method of documentation, and do you stick to this method consistently throughout your essay?**

8. **Does your bibliography mention all materials you have used? Does your list of references include all the works you have cited?**

---

[9] *Notes on the Preparation of Essays* provides more detailed information on spelling, splitting words, titles in texts, numbers in texts, and proper methods of quotation and documentation.

All bibliographies, lists of references, or lists of cited works should be arranged according to the conventions of documentation.

9. **Does your title page contain all the information your instructor needs?** Usually, the student's name and student number, the course name, the instructor's name, and the paper's submission date should appear with the title on an essay's title page. Try also to title your essays creatively. A good title is informative and thematic; it indicates the topic of the paper and something of the thesis as well. Two tantalizing yet informative titles are "Through the Glass Darkly: The Role of Windows in *The Watch That Ends the Night*" and "Taking Liberties: British Imperialism as a Cause of World War I."

Exercise Eighteen: Proofreading

The following paragraph contains sixteen errors that should have been caught by a careful proofreader. Try to find them all. It will probably be useful to read the passage aloud slowly.

> "Roughing It In the Bush," Susanna Moodies witty and moving book about her experiences in Upper Canada during the 1830s' seems to capture the essense of canadian life. However, were it not for the storytelling skillls of another writer, our beloved Susanna might never hae come to Canada. Susannas' husband Dunbar filled his book Ten Years in South Africa with with so many tales of danger and misshap that Susanna emphaticaly refused to accopany him to so terrofying and dangerous a country. It was unfortunate for the Moodies that Dunbar wrote so convincingly – they undoubtedly would have faired better there than they did in Canda.

Revising and Proofreading Using a Computer

There is no doubt that microcomputers have revolutionized the writing process; the ability to revise, proofread, and correct without having to handwrite an entirely new draft at each stage makes much more polished writing possible for undergraduates. However, any new technology demands new methods of approach and presents new problems. If you are composing your essay on a word processor, you will have to be alert not only to the many difficulties we have already discussed in this book, but also to a few new stylistic errors unique to computer-produced prose.

That the writing medium shapes the writing process has been discussed by Christina Haas and others. Haas concludes that not only do people who compose using word processors plan less than people who hand-write their texts, but that computers encourage "an over-attendance to low-level concerns."[10] Because word processors make it easy to fiddle with the sentences and paragraphs of essays, and since a computer's screen shows only a small portion of a complete essay at one time, students using computers to draft and revise often neglect the most significant improvements they can make to their papers. They spend their time endlessly tidying up sections of their work without discovering how these sections might be rearranged and more closely connected to make up a whole.

Even if you do use a computer to reorder the paragraphs of your essay, be aware that this is no different than a "scissors and paste" approach to revision. Granted, a computer allows you to rearrange your essay without re-typing it. But often the very fact that writers in a pre-computer world had to re-type the essays that they had reorganized encouraged more extensive revisions which promoted the unity and coherence of their final papers. You must work to achieve these qualities when you rearrange your essay on a computer. What emerges should not be choppy; the natural flow of the argument must be maintained. What you must do, therefore, is not simply put your ideas in the best possible order, but also work at reconstructing the logical connections between these ideas, and at making these connections apparent to your reader. It may be necessary to add a transitional sentence to some paragraphs; you may want to change the transitional words you have used to ones more appropriate to your new pattern of development. When you have finished, print a hard copy so that you can look through the whole paper to check for overall structure.

In fact, since the most effective method of ensuring that a paper still reads gracefully after it has been revised is to read it aloud, it is best to print a hard copy of your essay after each major revision. Reading from a computer screen is not a completely satisfactory method of checking an essay's style; you will be forced to pause, to disrupt the flow of your reading because a computer screen can display only a portion of your paper at a time. It is also a good idea to proofread from a hard copy, not only because errors are more easily spotted on a typewritten page, but

---

[10] Christina Haas, "How the Writing Medium Shapes the Writing Process: Effects of Word Processing on Planning," *Research in the Teaching of English* 23 (May 1989) 202.

because you can keep a record of errors corrected. Obviously, computers do not save trees.

Proofread what you think is your last printing of an essay thoroughly; a silent communion transpires between computer and printer wherein errors are slipped into a text that appears perfect in print and on the monitor. Watch in particular for errors in formatting: footnotes not indented, block quotations double-spaced, runaway underlining or italics. Instructors who have computers of their own are likely to be sympathetic about such technical slips, but they are still slips, and they certainly will not improve your grade. Better to kill another pine tree.

On the positive side, most computers have proofreading programmes that, when used properly, can be of tremendous assistance to you. Even the most rudimentary electronic typewriters now have dictionaries, and although they cannot solve all spelling problems, they can eliminate many typographical and human errors. Good spellers should use the computer dictionary to catch typos; these dictionaries make a cleaner essay possible for everyone. You should remember, however, that computer dictionaries cannot detect homonym mistakes, so if the confusion of "their," "there," and "they're" or "two," "too," and "to" is a problem, proofread for these variants.

New software can do much more than check spelling. There are sophisticated editing programmes that will analyze texts by counting the usual number of words in each sentence or the frequency with which the verb "to be" is used. These programmes often make suggestions about ways to revise writing. Remember, however, that software such as this can only detect and count the number of times certain character strings appear. A computer's evaluation of texts is quantitative, not qualitative; writers and readers must judge the value of writing by assessing whether or not its meaning is clearly and elegantly expressed.

A final note: procrastination is given new and vivid possibilities on a microcomputer. Lock away your chess and Pac-man software when you begin to write; otherwise, you may spend hours trying to "beat the computer." And don't use the revising capabilities of your computer as a means of avoiding the composition of new material; a polished, perfectly spelled introduction is worthless on its own. Last but not least, remember to "save" your work frequently. The excuse that your paper was destroyed by the computer is beginning to sound as threadbare to instructors as the invention that the family dog ate your final draft.

CHAPTER NINE
Conclusion

As a student, you have probably heard the teachers, parents, and other authority figures in your life lament that the younger generation does not know how to write, and that writing proficiency has declined dramatically since: (a) their childhood, (b) the beginning of the twentieth century, or (c) any other convenient date in the not-so-distant past. Do not allow these comments to make you feel inadequate, for the deterioration, if indeed it has taken place, is easily explained. The nature of communication itself has altered in the past several decades. The telephone has virtually eliminated the practice of letter writing, and the television, the practice of reading for information or entertainment. Writing and reading have become less important in our everyday lives, while other modes of communication have flourished. It is only natural, therefore, that the emphasis on fluency in other media has caused a decline in the acquisition of writing skills.

Nonetheless, those who lament the loss are justified. Difficult as the act of writing may be in a world where it is but infrequently performed, it is one means of communication that demands intense and committed engagement with a subject. Watching television is a passive pastime – the box supplies a set of words and images, and the audience receives them; one cannot stop for the activity of thinking critically without missing something. Conversation is active, but imprecise; here you always have the opportunity to backtrack, slow down, or question the speaker, but you also risk getting sidetracked. Writing is incisive and exact. To write an effective essay, a student must contemplate a topic, not merely long enough to form an opinion about it, but long enough to consider the other opinions possible, and to defend his or her stance. Such an act is exercise for the mind, and the inability to engage in it is correctly perceived as cause for alarm.

Furthermore, and more immediate to your purpose, at the university level the essay remains the primary medium for communication, precisely because it does engage the mind. Our continuing refrain throughout this book has therefore been to think your way through the essay. By this we mean not only thinking through the particular subject at hand, but also considering the essay as a subject in itself. Being aware of what an essay is, or can be, its principles of development, its voice and audience, takes the mystery out of determining "what the professor wants": not a particular point of view, but a productive method of approach.

Whether it be a first year paper or a doctoral thesis, your essay is seen as a contribution to the scholarly community, as "new thought" on a particular topic. It is your response to the material contemplated, for it is your perspective—your research, your ideas, your argument—that makes what you are writing "original" and "new." We stress the importance of a thesis to help you keep this notion of a personal contribution in mind; the thesis is the backbone of a paper because it supplies your rationale for writing and, without that rationale, that personal contribution, your essay will be nothing more than a recording of data.

An essay is not just an interaction between writer and subject, however; it is also an interaction between writer and reader. Once you have thought your own way through the subject, you must polish your prose through revision so that the ideas that seem patently obvious to you become as apparent to the reader. We find clarity in written work difficult to achieve because we are accustomed to communicating our ideas in conversation, where the oral cues of voice, gesture, pitch, and tone enhance our meaning. Much of this book is devoted to making you aware of the structural and contextual properties necessary in written work to compensate for the absence of those cues.

All essays need to be clear, but they cannot be reduced to standard patterns of development. Your main goal in essay writing should be to refine your thinking such that you can convey your ideas clearly to a reader, and if that end is achieved, almost any means are acceptable. Flexibility is the fundamental rule of composition; the moment you begin to think of the essay as a rigid structure, writing becomes difficult. You will have noticed that in our text we blithely ignore many of the traditional notions of formal writing. We use the first and second person. We end our sentences with prepositions, we start them with conjunctions, and we italicize occasionally to emphasize words. We compromise the seriousness of our endeavour by making the occasional joke. Stick to the conventions of form when they make meaning more clear (usually they will), and ignore them when you recognize that they will interfere with the force of your argument.

Writing essays is not easy, and writing books about writing essays is no piece of cake either. Often, during the composition of this book, we struggled with the difficulties of the sequential form of prose, knowing that the writing process we were describing could not be reduced to a step-by-step procedure. Sometimes you will write an outline after having completed a rough draft. Sometimes a flash of thought will necessitate a change of thesis late in the essay-writing process. The act of writing will make you think about your topic more deeply, and will take you in new directions. Permit yourself, therefore, to move freely when you write a paper: go backwards when you reconsider a concept, move sideways if interesting ideas beckon, jump ahead when fleeting insights demand to be recorded. And use our book freely as well. Do not feel that it is necessary to follow our advice from page one onwards: concentrate on what you need to know. Let your argument and your audience determine your direction, and you will have made good use of the opportunity the essay provides to think deeply into your subject, and to reveal that thought to your reader.

Appendices

APPENDIX A

Terms Commonly Used in Essay Topics

Analyze
— break something down into parts in order to understand its workings better by exploring relations between the parts or between the parts and the whole

Compare
— explore similarities

Contrast
— explore differences

Criticize
— give a reasoned judgement about the nature of the subject under discussion; might (or might not) involve evaluation of the accuracy or merit of the subject

Define
— give a clear meaning of the word or concept, setting out its limits in a given context

Describe
— characterize without critical judgement

Discuss
— examine an issue critically; sometimes involves responding to a given perspective, (dis)agreeing in whole or in part

Enumerate
— list concisely

Evaluate
— appraise carefully, looking at strengths and weaknesses, advantages and limitations

Explain
— account for, clarify the "how" and "why"

Illustrate
— make clear by means of concrete examples or specific instances

Interpret
— offer a perspective on a subject

Justify
— show grounds for conclusions; present convincing evidence

Outline
— arrange the main points and essential supporting points concisely and systematically; omit minor details

Prove
— using evidence and logical reasoning, verify a claim or hypothesis

Refute
— using evidence and logical reasoning, disprove the statement or claim made

Relate
— show connections and associations

Review
— survey something, often a book, and comment critically on it

State
— express the main point(s) clearly and succinctly

Summarize — present the main points in condensed form, omitting most details, illustrations, and elaborations

Trace — describe, in narrative sequence, the development of an event or instance beginning at a specified point, often the point of origin

APPENDIX B

Transitional Words and Phrases

1. *Adding Ideas*
again, also, and, and then, as well as, besides, equally important, finally, first (second, third, etc.), for one thing, further, furthermore, in addition, in the first place, last, likewise, more, moreover, next, nor, similarly, too

2. *Emphasizing Ideas*
above all, after all, equally important, especially, indeed, in fact, in particular, it is true, of course, most important, truly

3. *Illustrating Ideas*
an illustration of, for example, for instance, in other words, in particular, namely, specifically, such as, that is, thus, to illustrate

4. *Comparing Ideas*
in the same way, likewise, similarly

5. *Contrasting Ideas*
and yet, but, but at the same time, despite, even so, conversely, differently, for all that, however, in contrast, in spite of, nevertheless, notwithstanding, on the contrary, on the other hand, or, otherwise, rather, regardless, still, though, unfortunately, yet

6. *Showing Cause and Effect*
accordingly, as a result, consequently, for this purpose, for that reason, hence, otherwise, so, then, therefore, thereupon, thus, to this end, with this object

7. *Placing Ideas in Time*
again, already, always, at first, at least, at length, at once, at that time, at the same time, briefly, concurrently, during this time, earlier, eventually, finally, first (second, third, fourth, etc.), formerly,

gradually, immediately, in future, in the meantime, in the past, last, lately, later, meanwhile, next, never, now, once, presently, promptly, recently, shortly, simultaneously, so far, sometimes, soon, subsequently, suddenly, then, thereafter, until now

8. *Summarizing Ideas*
all in all, altogether, as has been noted, finally, in brief, in conclusion, in other words, in short, in simpler terms, in summary, on the whole, that is, to put it differently, to summarize

APPENDIX C

Conjunctions and Relative Pronouns

Conjunctions and relative pronouns can help you to establish the connection between clauses within a sentence.

1. *Subordinate Conjunctions*

   Contrasting Ideas
   although, even though, whereas, while

   Showing Cause and Effect
   because, since, so that

   Placing Ideas in Time
   after, afterward, as long as, as soon as, before, once, since, until, when, whenever, while

   Establishing Conditions
   assuming that, if, inasmuch as, insofar as, in case, in order that, provided that, so that, to the extent that, unless, whether

2. *Coordinate Conjunctions*

   and, or, for, nor, so, but, yet

3. *Relative Pronouns*

   who, whom, whose, which, that

APPENDIX D

Sample Essay A

The following essay was completed as a first year English assignment. It uses the endnoting/footnoting method of documentation.

Images and Gobbledegook:
Rain and Doubt in the Final Section of
T.S. Eliot's *The Waste Land*

In Joseph Heller's *Catch 22*, one of the air bases receives the message: "T.S. Eliot." This communication throws the entire military machine into confusion, as everyone tears out their hair trying to figure out what it could possibly mean. The message is in fact an answer to the question, "Who ever made any money by being a poet?" but several wild theories are proposed, and the original purpose of the message is never discovered. The episode is a humorous comment on the great twentieth-century poet. T.S. Eliot's work demands interpretation yet seems impervious to any final attempt to understand it. This is certainly the case with *The Waste Land*, his best-known and arguably most important work.[1]

Upon a rapid preliminary reading, in fact, *The Waste Land* appears to have no meaning at all. It is too obscure, too disjointed. Yet the unravelling of a single image proves to be the key to all the others, for the images are intermeshed to the extent that, upon closer examination, the poem resolves itself into a single image. The image is one of hopeless desolation and spiritual dryness. It is the image of the title—the waste land. The poem presents fragmented scenes of a purposeless, empty existence with no hope of renewal or resurrection. In the final section, as one might hope, Eliot talks about the rain that could bring relief to this waste land. Yet the Hindu thunder proverb that he offers is alien enough to a Western reader that this resurrection seems almost forced or artificial. The poem ends in a storm of broken images that reflects the whole poem, but fails to give a clear way out of the problems it presents. Thus, the hope offered seems hard to accept, when contrasted with the hard reality of the image of the waste land.

The last section, "What the Thunder Said," begins with the theme from the poem's title—the waste land. Eliot's footnote tells us that it is painted with a series of images that are actually parallel to one another: the journey to Emmaus from Luke, the journey to the Chapel Perilous from the Grail legend, an Antarctic expedition, and the decay of contemporary Eastern Europe.

The first stanza evokes the period after Gethsemane and Golgotha and before the Resurrection. There is no hope yet, no promise of resurrection. The lines still express the spiritual dryness that has filled the poem so far. The next two stanzas, which seem to refer to the journey to the Chapel Perilous, are dominated by dryness. From line 322 to line 359 the absence of water is mentioned eleven times, and direct reference to water is made frequently, emphasizing the need for relief from dryness. "Rock," "mountain," and "sand" instead make up the landscape, and the speaker prays for even the sound of water.

The next stanza begins "Who is the third who walks always beside you?" (360). Eliot's footnote recalls a phenomenon often observed by explorers in arctic regions: the feeling that someone else is walking beside you. This feeling could be hopeful, as it suggests that there is something else present here in the waste land that is not yet perceived. A more obvious interpretation of this stanza is as an allusion to the journey to Emmaus (Luke 24: 13-16). This reference is a little more hopeful than the first mention of Christ, for it suggests that hope and resurrection are indeed at hand, merely as yet unnoticed.

This spark of hope is not reflected in the next stanza. "What is that sound high in the air" (367) asks the first line. Then "Who are those hooded hordes swarming/Over endless plains . . . What is the city over the mountains/Cracks and reforms and bursts" (369-73). Eliot hints in two of his notes at Eastern Europe, but the stanza itself ends with a more universal list of cities: "Jerusalem Athens Alexandria/Vienna London" (375-6). Indeed the city is too easily any city. The "hooded hordes . . . stumbling in cracked earth" (370) are too easily all of us. Eastern Europe might be a good example of what Eliot calls "the waste land," but we can see that the waste land extends to include the world.

By the sixth stanza, the nature of the waste land has changed from dryness to emptiness and desolation. Strangely, there is music, "fiddled whisper music" (379), and bats whistling. There are even voices singing, but their songs rise out of "empty cisterns and exhausted wells" (385).

If the imagery of stanza six is bleak, that of stanza seven has become almost frightening. What catches the eye are the "decayed hole," the "moonlight," the "tumbled graves," and the line "There is the empty chapel, only the wind's home. It has no windows and the door swings" (390). As far as scary images go, these are really rather hackneyed, but this stanza seems to refer to the journey to the Chapel Perilous, in which case it is all merely an illusion: the final test. Indeed, the second half of the stanza dispels the uneasiness and even offers hope. "Dry bones can harm no one" (391), it says. The cock crows, signalling dawn and safety from evil. And then, after three hundred and ninety-four lines of dryness, the final line of the stanza, "Bringing rain" (395), makes the reader sit up attentively.

Yet, the positive imagery is not given with confidence. The comment that accompanies each component of the Hindu moral is disturbing. To *datta,* Eliot asks "[W]hat have we given?" (402). Giving is crucial but excruciatingly difficult. It must be "[t]he awful daring of a moment's surrender" (404), a total thing. "By this, and this only, we have existed" (406), he says, and not by what is usually thought of as giving. The example that is given of such empty gestures are the obviously hollow gifts of a will. The tense used in this line ("we have existed") seems to suggest that people do achieve this act, but the difficulty of the achievement and the desolate tone of the passage do not help the reader to believe what the stanza implies.

To *dayadhvam,* Eliot suggests that we are all locked within ourselves and unable to sympathize. In his note to line 412 ("I have heard the key"), he quotes F.H. Bradley's *Appearance and Reality* which argues that external sensations are as private as thoughts or feelings, so that the whole world is particular and private to each soul.[2] The way individuals experience the world, Eliot believes, causes the "locking" up of persons within themselves. "We think of the key, each in his prison/Thinking of the key, each confirms a prison" (414-15). Realizing our imprisonment only confirms our being shut off from the outside world.

To *damyata,* the poet seems more positive, devoting five lines to describing a boat responding "gaily" to control, and linking the boat to the heart. But then there is a break which ends with "I sat upon the shore/Fishing, with the arid plain behind me/Shall I at least set my lands in order?" (424-6). The image from Psalm 137 ("By the rivers of Babylon, there we sat down, yea, we wept"), which has already been used, immediately recalls despair. Why? The speaker sits with the waste land at his back, fishing, or searching for something, and asks how far he can control. His question might also be "why bother?" With all the terrible emptiness of the waste land welling up behind, why bother trying to control? The "rain" that Eliot finally sprinkles on the waste land thus does more to show the extent of its dryness than to offer hope for a resurrection.

The remaining eight lines are so obscure and fragmented as to represent *The Waste Land* in miniature:

London Bridge is falling down falling down falling down
Poi s'ascose nel foco che gli affina
Quando fiam uti chelidon - O swallow swallow
Le Prince d'Aquitaine à la tour abolie
These fragments I have shored against my ruins
Why then Ile fit you. Hieronymo's mad againe.
Datta. Dayadhvam. Damyata.
                    Shantih shantih shantih (427-34)

This section contains references to seven other works and uses five languages, including English, from three different eras. The line that one tends to grab onto is the only one in modern English prose: "These fragments I have shored against my ruins" (431). This line could help explain this section — fragments that the speaker has found to hold onto. Indeed, the line probably refers to the whole poem — fragments shored against the hopelessness of the waste land.

The London Bridge line is the culmination of a repeated image in this section, of the waste land as an urban landscape. In the final section, we have the city that "cracks and reforms and bursts" (373), "falling towers" (374), towers "upside down in air" (383), and the ruined chapel from stanza seven. London Bridge was so large that it was its own community, and in the image of a whole village literally falling, Eliot completes his description of the spiritual bankruptcy of the urban world.

The line from *Purgatorio*, *"Poi s'ascose nel foco che gli affina"* (428), translates to mean "he hid himself in the fire which refines them."[3] Here is something positive: in the fire, one may find regeneration. The next line, with its plaintive call, is sad, but sadness is still positive in the sense that it is *something*, unlike the emptiness that most of the poem expresses. It also does express hope for renewal: "When shall I be as the swallow?"[4]

So, in a confused way, the last eight lines do express some hope and some direction. Eliot ends by re-stating the guidelines from the Hindu thunder parable and then giving the Hindu version of the peace: "Shantih shantih shantih" (434). These are all profound-sounding words with heavy significance. Yet they are so foreign to the Western reader that one has difficulty in accepting them on a basic, instinctual level. In the end, the reader is left wondering if this is a way out or merely another one of the broken fragments that make up Eliot's waste land.

Notes

[1] T.S. Eliot, *The Waste Land. The Norton Anthology of English Literature,* eds. M.H. Abrams et al., 5th ed., vol. 2 (N. Y.: Norton, 1974) 2180-2196. All references in the text are to this edition and are noted by line number.

[2] M.H. Abrams et al., eds., *The Norton Anthology of English Literature,* 5th ed., vol.2 (N.Y.: Norton, 1974) 2195, n. 8.

[3] Abrams et al., eds., 2195, n. 4.

[4] Abrams et al., eds., 2195, n. 5.

Bibliography

Eliot, T.S. *The Waste Land. The Norton Anthology of English Literature.* Eds. M.H. Abrams et al. 5th ed. Vol. 2. N. Y.: Norton, 1974. 2180-2196.

Sample Essay B

The following essay was submitted in a first year politics course. It uses the form of parenthetical documentation preferred in political science.

Interest Groups in Canada and the United States
A Comparative Study

Gabriel Almond defines interest groups as organizations which:

> articulate political demands in the society, seek support for these demands among other groups by advocacy and bargaining and attempt to transform these demands into authoritative public policy by influencing the choice of political personnel and the various processes of public policy making and enforcement (Almond, quoted in Van Loon and Whittington 297).

Interest groups are considerably more predominant in the States than in Canada. The sheer number of lobby groups in the States, estimated to be approximately 20,000, suggests that the American political environment is extremely conducive to successful lobbying. In comparison, pressure groups seem not nearly as numerous in Canada, partly because their activities are "not highly visible to the untrained eye" (Landes 364), but primarily because the political environment is less opportune. Interest groups in general are better off in the United States; however, when a public interest group is working for social change, there are instances when the Canadian system may be a preferable working environment.

One factor that allows pressure groups to proliferate in the U.S. and to be held back in Canada is the different political cultures of the two countries. Americans place a great emphasis on being independent, voicing and fighting for individual concerns, and are also "inherently suspicious of political power and its uses" (Landes 234). This deep-rooted belief in popular sovereignty is the basis for their political organization and culture. Thus, in a society which promotes public participation, lobby groups are a natural concept. Canadian culture, on the other hand, is characterized by parliamentary sovereignty. Canadian citizens look toward, and even rely on, the elitist authorities to provide them with "peace, order, and good government." Interest groups, which often must challenge authority, are not always viewed benignly and may not always receive the same amount of support as their counterparts to the south do.

The differing political attitudes are reflected in the two countries' political structures and help account for interest groups' success in each. The Canadian polity does not provide many lobbying opportunities for interest groups due to its political design. Because cabinet ministers devise programs and policies based on the advice of their internal agencies, most pressure groups' strategies involve lobbying only the bureaucracy and the executive. A bill that gets placed before the House of Commons is not likely to be rejected (especially if there is a majority government), since doing so would threaten dissolution of the House. Lobbyists can try to introduce a bill through a Member of Parliament, but M.P.s are limited by party discipline, and the Private Members' bills introduced are considered only in the order they appear, are often not debated, and are rarely passed. "Most interest groups realize that policy is not made in Parliament and that lobbying M.P.s when legislation is already before the House is futile" (Van Loon and Whittington 306). Therefore, they concentrate on the two critical points where they can possibly have a serious impact (the cabinet ministers and the relevant government departments in the bureaucracy).

The American political system is much more open to interest groups, since many more opportunities to exert pressure exist. The powers of the executive and legislature are separate and party discipline is weak, and "[t]his fragmentation [of power] exposes all the facets and levels of government to interest group activity and also focuses much of such activity on the legislative process" (Holtzman 58). In contrast to M.P.s, legislators, unconstrained by party discipline, can represent the interests of their constituents and lobby groups in Congress freely. Not only do interest groups make use of this access point; "communication from interest groups [is also] considered functional to the legislators' ability to operate effectively in the congressional system" (Holtzman 75). Interest groups need Congress and vice versa.

The U.S. federal system is not only more accessible because it offers more places for exerting influence, but also because lobbyists are *expected* to contribute directly in the policy-making procedure. For a long time, interest groups have been regularly included in the bargaining process that takes place in conference committees and throughout the legislative process (Oleszek 189). In Canada the situation is almost the reverse; the influence of interest groups on committees is minimal. Van Loon and Whittington note that "when legislation is before the House Standing Committee, it is expected that all interested groups will present briefs. However, one would be hard pressed to find recent examples where these presentations have done much to modify legislation" (311). A Royal Commission also provides an opportunity for concerned groups to present their cases; ultimately however the commission's report "usually draws more heavily from its research staff than it does from private submissions" (Van Loon and Whittington 311). That the Canadian system is much less receptive to the information provided by interest groups, while Congress relies quite heavily on the valuable political information and social perspectives that lobbyists offer, is again a reflection of the different political cultures.

With respect to citizens' rights, the United States has traditionally guaranteed the right to "free speech, press and assembly" through the First Amendment, as well as the right to "petition the Government for a redress of grievances" (Landes 357). These rights have allowed American lobbyists to go to court to gain access to government policies and to protest against those decisions that have already gone against them (Landes 364). In Canada it is just recently that lobby groups have gained legitimacy in using judiciary methods and litigation as a lobbying technique. Before 1982 and the Charter of Rights and Freedoms, lobby groups had no legal grounds upon which to challenge the government. Today they can use Section 7 and 15 as an appeal. Nonetheless, many groups are still not being heard in court due to their lack of "standing" (a measure that has been put in place to regulate the rush of interest group cases). Presumably the courts will eventually be able to accommodate the rush, so that the standing barrier can be removed, and interest groups in Canada will obtain access to the judiciary method of lobbying.

Even with the potential for equal access to the courts, Canadian pressure groups are often at a disadvantage. Information is extremely important when fighting for one's rights. In the U.S., citizens and lobby groups have access to government documents which they can use to scrutinize and challenge their government's policies. In Canada, on the other hand, the "Official Secrets Act prohibits disclosure of government information, even if that information has nothing to do with national security" (Landes 219). Canadians are thus barred from obtaining the information they need (Howard 132) which puts them at a distinct disadvantage when trying to bring their government to court.

Funding is another important prerequisite for the success of interest groups. Money is always needed to carry out research, publish findings, file court cases, hire lawyers, raise public awareness through education, and, in general, to fight effectively for a cause. In Canada, receiving funding from the government is difficult because of the self-protective nature of government funding policies. Ross Howard notes that in 1978, the federal government even "threatened to remove tax-exempt status from numerous reputable groups . . . because their activities included criticism of existing federal policies" (137). For those groups who receive funding, in most cases the monies "specifically do not include courtroom and hearing board appearances" (Howard 137).

In contrast, interest groups in the States receive comparatively generous financial backing from their government because policy makers and high officials realize that "without the well-researched and well-organized comment and analysis by public interest groups, issues [do] not receive a truly full and fair airing" (Howard 139). Federal agencies "not only have the freedom to fund citizen groups but also the responsibility and duty to do so, as a matter of standard procedure" (Howard 137). Dollars, it turns out, can be a major factor in determining an interest group's success, especially in judiciary challenges.

Money is also a very powerful lobbying tool in terms of of Policy Action Committees. PACs are organizations or groups which give work and money directly to a particular candidate with the expectation that the politician will, in turn, advocate for that group's concern. In the States, laws passed during the 1970s have favoured PACs and thus allowed them to flourish. Today PACs have "become the most important source for interest group campaign contributions and the largest single source of campaign fundraising for many seeking legislative office" (Landes 359). In the U.S., they are a widely used and effective lobbying method for interest groups with money. Conversely, Canadians have tried to hinder the growth of PACs through Bill C-169 in 1984, which was "to prevent groups other than parties from spending funds during an election campaign" (Landes 365). The bill was challenged shortly after passing and put on hold. If this bill were to remain in place, some shelter would be given to interest groups with sparse funds, but the lobbying technique of many others would be hindered. The effectiveness and influence of PACs, however, will always remain less in Canada, regardless of Bill C-169, because they are limited by the strength of parliamentary parties and party discipline.

It is primarily due to the limited number of PACs that a public interest group fighting for a particular social concern may in some instances prefer to deal with the Canadian system. Recently, with the increase in the number of interest groups, a new phenomenon has occurred where lobby groups must now compete with each other. Public interest groups (in both countries) are often small in number, low on funds, and not well-organized. Obviously they are at a disadvantage should they be placed in competition with big business lobby groups which are well-funded, well-organized and can write off lobbying costs as company expenditures. Unfortunately, public interest groups' campaigns often stand to affect big business negatively and the two come head to head. For example, an environmental organization that wants the government to impose stricter standards for SO emissions from industrial smoke stacks threatens those companies that would have to implement a proper cleaning system. The companies could stand to lose substantial amounts of money and would counter with a lobby of their own. Small pressure groups often do not have enough funds to keep their heads above water, let alone counter the influence of PACs from big companies. In Canada, public interest groups might not encounter this potentially overwhelming competition, due to the comparably limited number and strength of PACs here.

Furthermore, while pressure groups do not receive as much funding or access to information here as in the States, the relatively socialist political attitude in Canada may compensate somewhat for those public interest groups that are reasonably well-off. Our citizens expect the government to provide a basic standard of living for all individuals and to assume responsibility for aiding the less able. Traditionally, we have not been driven by the goal of individual freedom to the same extent as Americans have. Competition and big business are very important aspects of their society. An illustration of this dichotomy is our national health insurance (provided to all Canadian citizens by the government) versus American medicare (a private medical insurance sold by large companies to those who want and can afford it) in the States. If Canadian citizens expect their government to be responsible for adopting and enforcing laws that preserve or better the public's health and well-being, politicians, who are citizens too, may be more receptive to the social concerns of public interest groups, especially since Canadian politicians do not live with the fear that their inability to win PAC support would mean that they could not afford to mount an adequate campaign (as does happen in the States) (Conway 129).

This receptiveness could work together well with another potentially positive aspect of the Canadian system. If a Canadian public interest group is successful in influencing policy before it enters the House, then that policy will almost certainly be passed and become law. In the United States, an interest group may succeed in gaining the support of all the legislature but may receive mighty opposition from the executive, or vice versa. Particularly with the influence of PACs, a public interest group's policy may have an incredibly difficult time getting through.

The United States today is characterized by an environment which protects and nurtures the various interest groups within it. The political culture, government structure, and entrenched rights and freedoms together create what seems to be a haven for lobbying organizations. Canada has always been regarded in an opposite light. Its closed government, lack of access and funding, and low respect for lobbying has hindered pressure groups from exerting the influence they might have in the States. With the Charter of Rights and Freedoms, Canada now has started to open its doors and allow pressure groups more areas in which they may fight their battles. Although we are still behind in using the valuable knowledge interest groups can give us and in accepting their worth, perhaps Canada, because of its socialist attitudes, provides a climate whereby interest groups stand a better chance of reaching their goals.

Works Cited

Berry, Jeffrey M. *Lobbying for the People: The Political Behaviour of Public Interest Groups*. Princeton, N.J.: Princeton UP, 1977.

Conway, M. Margaret. "PACs, the New Politics and Congressional Campaigns." *Interest Group Politics*. Eds. Allan J. Cigler and Burdett A. Loomis. Washington, D.C.: CQ P, 1983.

Holtzman, Abraham. *Interest Groups and Lobbying*. New York: Macmillan, 1966.

Howard, Ross. *Poisons in Public: Case Studies of Environmental Pollution in Canada.* Toronto: James Lorimer, 1980.

Landes, Ronald G. *The Canadian Polity: A Comparative Introduction.* 2nd ed. Scarborough: Prentice-Hall, 1987.

Oleszek, Walter J. *Congressional Procedures and the Policy Process.* Washington, D.C.: CQ P, 1978.

Pross, A. Paul. *Pressure Group Behaviour in Canadian Politics.* Toronto: McGraw-Hill Ryerson, 1975.

Van Loon, Richard, and Michael S. Whittington. *The Canadian Political System: Environment, Structure and Processes.* Toronto: McGraw-Hill, 1971.

Sample Essay C

The following essay was written for an upper year biology course. It uses the parenthetical method of reference preferred by biology.

The Origins of Distemper Virus in Harbour Seals

All living organisms are susceptible to the effects of pathenogenic microorganisms. Perhaps the most interesting, and least understood, of all these microorganisms is the virus, since it must be cultured in living tissue rather than on a culture medium. Virology is, of course, best studied in animals since a complete study may then be performed, and such a study may be carried out relatively easily if the virus has already been identified. This has not, however, been the case with the harbour seal (*Phoca vitulina*) populations in the North and Baltic Sea areas. Recently, they have been plagued by a viral epidemic which has attracted the attention of scientists who have wanted both to identify the virus and to determine its origins.

Seventeen years ago, the Netherlands set up an institution, The Pieterburn Center, in an attempt to halt a drastically declining seal population. The institution captured orphaned seals, raised them, and later returned the seals to the natural environment. This program had tremendous success and the seal population increased significantly until about a year ago, when concern arose that more than 90% of these captured seal pups were suffering from an unknown and often fatal disease (Dickson, 1988a, p. 893). Estimates suggest that this disease had already killed approximately 9000 of the 15000 to 16000 harbour seals previously found along the North Sea coasts of the Netherlands, West Germany, Denmark, Sweden, and Norway (Dickson, 1988b, p. 1284). This disease was also spreading among the seal populations of the United Kingdom.

Based on information gathered in post mortem examinations and previous viral epidemics, The Pieterburn Center was able to determine that herpes and picornaviral infections were present in the dead seal bodies. However, some symptoms the seals exhibited did not coincide with the symptoms produced by either of these viruses. The infected seals suffered from heavy inflammation of the lungs (usually resulting in death from pneumonia), encephalitis (inflammation of the brain), peritonitis (inflammation of the abdominal cavity membrane), osteomyelitis (suppurative inflammation of the bone), premature abortion, deep skin lesions, and histopathological brain lesions (Dickson, 1988a, p. 893). Vedder, a scientist for The Pieterburn Center, concluded that the disease the seals had contracted must be more complicated than originally thought (Dickson, 1988a, p. 893).

As it turned out, Vedder was correct in this conclusion. Shortly after the herpes virus and picornavirus were isolated, a third virus, determined to be the one causing the problem, was isolated in mid-August 1988 (Dickson, 1988b, p. 1284). It was identified as either the canine distemper virus (CDV) or a mutated form called morbillivirus. The herpes and picornavirus were now considered secondary infections as a result of a depressed immune system.

Distemper, a morbillivirus ranging in size from 115 to 160 millimicrons (Gillespie and Carmichael, 1968, p. 114), is a very contagious airborne viral infection that passes out of the body through various secretions and excretions. The virus is almost identical to that of measles and is thought to have ribonucleoprotein as the internal component. Distemper will survive away from a host cell temporarily if the environment is cold and dry. It is not very tolerant to a warm moist environment and dies rather quickly in such conditions. For example, distemper will only survive between 3 and 20 hours in an incubator at 20 degrees Celsius (Gillespie and Carmichael, 1968, p. 114). The CDV adapted egg virus will tolerate pH conditions between 4.4 and 10.4 although the optimum pH is between 8 and 9 (Gillespie and Carmichael, 1968, p. 114). There are also some chemical compounds that will kill CDV. These compounds include 0.75% phenol, 0.2% roccal, and 0.1% formalin (Gillespie and Carmichael, 1968, p. 114).

The treatment presently used to combat distemper is relatively simple under certain conditions. First of all, large doses of distemper antibodies and canine gamma globulin are injected into the animal. The next step is to limit the possibility of secondary bacterial infections by adjusting the body fluid levels and "controlling nervous manifestations" (Siegmund, 1973, p. 312). This is achieved by administering "antibiotics, electrolyte solutions, protein hydrolyscites, dietary supplements, antipyretics, nasal preparations and analgesics" (Siegmund, 1973, p. 312).[1] The animal must also be kept in a warm and relatively humid environment. Most important, the animal must be under close serveillance and kept comfortable.

It is clear that much care must be given to an animal with CDV. For this reason, such treatment is neither practical nor applicable to the wild seals presently suffering from the virus. Because the seals cannot practicably be treated, scientists need to understand both the origins of this disease and the reasons for the seals contracting it upon exposure. Any preventative measures that can be taken depend on this information.

One of the first theories about the origin of the virus came from the Department of Immunobiology at the National Institute of Public Health and Environmental Hygiene at Bilthorn in the Netherlands. According to the Institute, the virus may have been introduced by harp seals mostly found in Greenland, since they had been seen much farther south than normal in 1988 (Dickson, 1988a, p. 894). The second and much stronger theory comes from John Baker, a veterinary pathologist specializing in seal diseases at Britain's Liverpool University (Dickson, 1988b, p. 1284). He theorizes that the CDV originated in an outbreak among the Arctic foxes on Baffin Island. These infected foxes then migrated across to Greenland and spread the virus to the huskies last winter. As a result of this epidemic among the huskies, many of these animals died, and there are reports of some of the carcasses being thrown into the sea. Since the sea is a relatively cold environment, and seals spend much time in the water, this would explain how so many seals contracted the virus at the same time.

The last problem to be addressed is why the seals contracted the virus or did not have the immunity to stop the infection in the first place. One strong theory is that there is a direct link between an increasing amount

---

[1] A point of clarification: antibiotics are administered solely for bacterial infections as they are useless against a virus. Only a preventative treatment of vaccination, resulting in partial immunity, will stop a virus. Once a virus has been contracted, the best that can be done is to treat the symptoms.

of pollution in the North and Baltic Seas and the rate of depression of the immune systems of the seals (Dickson, 1988a, p. 893). The pollution that most concerns the scientists is the discharge of toxic chemicals, and of polychlorinated biphenyls (PCBs) in particular. Minnie Courtney, a marine biologist at the University of London's Queen Mary College, has performed widespread studies to determine the effects of organochlorines on the environment. One of the results she discovered was that high concentrations of PCBs were found in the seals' bodies. PCBs are known to reduce fertility significantly. This reduced fertility would have a drastic effect on population when compounded with the viral infection. Furthermore, Ottmar Wassermann, professor of toxicology at the University of Kiel, notes that PCBs have been shown to impair the immune system in other mammals (Dickson, 1988a, p. 894). Wassermann states that, without firm data, "we have to take the scientifically clear evidence we have from other mammals and apply it to seals" (Dickson, 1988a, p. 894).

PCBs, however, are not the only chemical of concern; dioxins, which will also impair the immune systems of mammals, appear to pose a problem in very low concentrations (Dickson, 1988a, p. 894). Albert Osterhaus probably sums up the dilemma about pollution best when he says, "We do not need pollution as an explanation; but the extent and the seriousness of the spread of the disease could well have been aggravated by a malfunction of the immune system in the seals" (Dickson, 1988b, p. 1284).

Although much information has been discovered about this morbillivirus, there is still more research to be done. All countries, not only those with seals, have a vested interest in defeating this virus because the exact nature of the mutation is not understood. Until it is, this virus could have even more drastic and devastating effects upon this ecosphere. If a polluted environment is capable of lowering the immune system of seals such that they are able to contract this CDV and manifest the disease, we cannot know whether the same situation will not arise with other species.

As all marine organisms are dependant on water for their oxygen and food, they will be exposed constantly to the virus. Although such organisms as plankton or fish may not be able to manifest the disease, they could act as carriers of the virus to animals higher in the food chain. The higher order animals that appear to be most affected are the mammals and birds. The obvious example for the mammals is of course the harbour seal. As for the birds, the rapid decline in the seabird population may or may not be related to that of the seals; research has yet to be done. If the two are related, however, one might suspect that fish are carrying the virus as this is the staple of both animals' diets.

If smaller organisms, such as plankton, are able to act as carriers, another mammal may also be at great risk. Many whales feed on plankton while other toothed whales will feed on seals. The quantity of food required by these giants, and the fact that they live in the water, suggests they may be very susceptible to this CDV. If this disease were to be manifested in the whale population, there might be no possible way of controlling it, because of the great distances that whales travel.

The ramifications of the canine distemper virus or its mutated form are obviously extensive. It is therefore clear that some action is necessary. Scientists across Europe and Canada are working at this problem from all sides. With the discovery of the virus responsible, a vaccine will eventually be developed. Institutions such as The Pieterburn Center working with wild animals will be administering this vaccine to the animals with which they come in contact. It is very doubtful, however, that any large scale vaccination will ever take place in the natural environment. These animals will just have to depend on natural immunity being passed genetically to the next generation.

References

BURNET, F.M. 1955. Principles of animal virology. Academic Press, New York.

DICKSON, D. 1988a. Mystery disease strikes Europe's seals. Science 241: 893-895.

DICKSON, D. 1988b. Canine distemper may be killing North Sea seals. Science 241: 1284.

GILLESPIE, J.H. and CARMICHAEL, L.E. 1968. Viral diseases. *In* Canine medicine. *Edited by* E.J. Catcott. First Catcott Edition. American Veterinary Publications, Santa Barbara, California. pp. 111-129.

KENNEDY, S., et al. 1988. Confirmation of cause of recent seal deaths. Nature 335: 404.

OSTERHAUS, A.D.M.E. and VEDDER, E.J. 1988. Identification of virus causing recent seal deaths. Nature 335: 20.

PELCZAR, M.J. 1972. Microbiology. 3rd Ed. McGraw-Hill, New York.

SIEGMUND, O.H., Ed. 1973. Canine distemper. *In* The Merck veterinary manual: a handbook of diagnosis and therapy for the veterinarian. 4th Ed. Merck & Co., Rashway, N.J. pp. 311-313.

Answer Key and Instructor's Guide

CHAPTER ONE
No exercises

CHAPTER TWO – Topic to Thesis

Exercise One: Narrowing the Topic
This exercise works best with a group of students: each individual adds
his or her own expertise about the topic at hand. Try narrowing each
topic first for a 5000 word essay, then for a 2500 word essay.

Exercise Two: Recasting the Topic in Question Form
Try asking why, where, when, how, and who questions of each topic.

Exercise Three: Key Words and Concepts
Students should note the following key words.
1. negative, environmental, consequences, economic advantages,
   implementation, advanced technology, vis-a-vis
2. commodification, virtue, modern
3. Treaty of Westphalia, Thirty Years' War, religious conflicts,
   Reformation, Counter-Reformation
4. methodological, Canadian settlement patterns, staples thesis, Innis,
   Creighton
5. world view, thematic reach, theatre of the absurd

Exercise Four: Subdividing the Topic
1. This question is asking the student to explain why Canada's economic
   system seems to cause either high inflation or massive unemployment and whether there are any solutions to the problem. One section
   of the essay would need to explain the system; another would evaluate
   it. In the process of evaluation, the final two questions would be
   answered.
2. The overall question in this topic is the first command: discuss the
   social effects of the Industrial Revolution in Britain. The questions
   which follow are prompts to help the student explore the topic fully;
   they also suggest that a narrative approach would be appropriate.

Exercise Five: Breaking Up the Topic

1. Students might want to look at four specific changes, and then at how these changes have affected specific cities. Another possibility would be to look at one change in spatial patterns and to see how it manifested itself in a city from each region of Canada.
2. The student might want to decide on particular instances of "violence" and "cooperation" as foci, and build the paper around them.

Exercise Six: Finding a Position

1. Solar energy safer, nuclear cheaper; solar energy safer and cheaper; nuclear energy safer and cheaper; solar energy cheaper, nuclear safer
2. Yes, no, in some circumstances, only in urban centres, important but not necessary, etc.

Exercise Seven: Brainstorming
No definite answers

Exercise Eight: Topic to Thesis Statement
No definite answers

Exercise Nine: Sample Thesis Statements
Note that, as is often the case in matters of essay writing, the sample thesis statements are not simply right or wrong. Some seriously flawed statements contain the germ of a good thesis; some strong statements could be improved upon.

1. Restates the topic (1)
2. Good cause and effect thesis statement; might be narrowed geographically either to Europe or North America (2)
3. Too broad (2); try narrowing each key concept in the statement
4. Basically a good statement but a bit wordy (5)
5. Restates the topic (1), and even as a topic is much too broad; as a self-evident proposition it fails the "so what" test (7, and most of the others as well)
6. In this form, "sensational" (6) and therefore not subject to proof; needs to be recast in the language of rational argument
7. Does not convey the priorities of the argument (7); general statement followed by unimportant details; moreover, statement hinges on a false analogy: commercial vs. natural food processing

8. Wordy (5); condense to single sentence: "Bees communicate by performing dance-like motions which provide information about the direction and distance of nectar from the hive."
9. Strong statement: note "although" clause and clincher statement at the end
10. Strong statement
11. Cryptic (4). Is this a philosophy essay? biology?
12. Too wordy (5); contains a reasonable argument but needs to be made more concise
13. Narrowly factual (6)
14. Strong statement
15. As stated, not subject to proof (6); recast in demonstrable form
16. Might be a good introductory statement, but not a thesis (1); thesis should go beyond statement to answer the question
17. Vague language; to an extent defines the prison in terms of itself ("caged mentally"); "frustrated lives" not explained adequately

CHAPTER THREE – Research

Exercise One: Choosing Your Research Direction

1. Does demand research. Government documents useful; interviews with workers and management useful; documents developed by lobby groups and NGOs a good source; current books and articles. Problems: may be difficult to obtain government documents – some will be confidential; accessibility a problem with private sources as well; currency a problem since information in field is continually changing
2. Does demand research. Read closely the texts of these authors and their biographies; consider secondary sources which evaluate these historians' works. Problems: time constraints – you will need to make choices about which primary texts to read
3. Does demand research. Could look at books and articles on the subject, but statistical research would be more useful. Taxation laws might help. Problems: might be difficult to obtain necessary information from Statistics Canada; currency of information is an issue; masses of data to process; need to define "significant" in order to limit research

4. Does demand research. Would need to look at lyrics of popular songs, musical theory, psychological studies of music. Problems: need to define "audience" (this might be tricky); problems with gauging popularity — different sources will use different indices
5. Does not necessarily demand research — just lots of thinking. Student might want to look at by-laws, court rulings, etc.
6. Does not demand secondary research: student need only focus on *The Lost Salt Gift of Blood*

CHAPTER FOUR — Reading

Exercise One: Reading for Detailed Understanding
Instructors may find this a useful exercise at the beginning of term to encourage active reading.

Exercise Two: Reading for General Knowledge
This exercise works well as a classroom activity. The instructor can bring in a selection of books, give the students fifteen minutes to read them, and then ask each member of the class to report on what he or she has learned.

Exercise Three: Critical Reading
Lots of room for discussion with this exercise. The initial task is to determine your own bias: which argument are you more sympathetic toward? Why? Students should see that the first selection is strongly biased against terrorist methods of protest and that the latter editorial is decidedly anti-American. They will also note the assumption in the first editorial that legitimate governments in power cannot be seen as terrorist, and the inverse assumption in the second editorial. They can proceed from there to find instances of up-labelling and down-labelling (navel-gazing vs. Rambo style), figurative language (Porsche-sized missiles, spill the blood), and unsupported generalizations. The exercise can occupy up to an hour of classroom time with an enthusiastic class.

CHAPTER FIVE — Notetaking

Exercise One: Notetaking
1. Missing editors; not arranged in exact bibliographic order. Correct form: Hall, David. "Clifford Sifton and Canadian Indian Administration, 1896-1905." *As Long as the Sun Shines and the Water Flows: A Reader in Canadian Native Studies.* Eds. Ian Getty and Antoine Lussier. Vancouver: U of British Columbia P, 1983.
2. Paraphrasing is weak: large chunks are taken directly from original text. Note could cause student to plagiarize
3. Fine, although Hall is not completely critical of Sifton's policies
4. Quotation is fine, but note is missing page number
5. Note needs to attribute information properly, both to Hall and to Sifton

Exercise Two: Paraphrasing
1. Fine, though not complete; no reference to the reasons for aid being offered
2. O.K. although one might question whether the late 1950s means 1955-60
3. Not precise enough, especially in terms of dates
4. Sentence follows syntax of original too closely
5. Fine

Exercise Three: Plagiarism
1. Depends too heavily on syntax from original source
2. Fine
3. Page reference should be cited
4. Fine

CHAPTER SIX — Prewriting

Exercise One: Free-writing
Good classroom exercise. Students may want to begin every writing session with a twenty minute free-writing period.

Exercise Two: Methods of Organization

Try not to struggle for accuracy when doing this exercise; that will only slow you down. Make up ridiculous thesis statements — the Fathers of Confederation came together as a result of the moon being in Cancer — to see how you would use different methods of development to explore the thesis.

Exercise Three: Creating the Outline

The subsections of Part III, particularly #1, are not very well-explained: how do the references to literary works function? The student might have forgotten the point to be made about these by the time he or she was writing. The outline demonstrates the thesis clearly and the mini-theses work well. Students might want to think about the possibilities of a descriptive rather than narrative method of development. How would a different method alter the outline?

Exercise Four: Creating the Reverse Outline

Sample Essay B on lobby groups or Sample Essay C on harbour seals would be appropriate for this exercise.

Exercise Five: Checking the Reverse Outline

Students should watch in particular for the method of development used in the sample essay. There are several plausible alternatives to the method of arrangement used in the paper. Also, consider the rhetorical arrangement. Is there one? How could it be changed to help defend the student's thesis?

Exercise Six: Checking the Outline

Keep your outlines. When an essay is returned to you, check the outline against the professor's comments. Students often repeat the same mistakes in organization, so watch for recurring patterns of error.

CHAPTER SEVEN — Drafting

No exercises

CHAPTER EIGHT – Revision

Exercise One: Gender-Neutral Language
Several variations of the following answers are possible.

1. Narcissism represents the psychological dimension of this dependence. Notwithstanding occasional illusions of omnipotence, the validation of the self-esteem of narcissists depends on others. They cannot live without an admiring audience. Their apparent freedom from family ties and institutional constraints does not free them to stand alone or to glory in individuality. On the contrary, it contributes to insecurity, which they can overcome only by seeing their "grandiose self" reflected in the attentions of others, or by attaching themselves to those who radiate celebrity, power, and charisma. For narcissists, the world is a mirror, whereas the rugged individualist saw it as an empty wilderness to be shaped to his or her own design.

2. Being read fairy tales by a parent is one of the most enriching experiences in childhood. First, the mere presence of a parent is important. Reading is one of many ways in which special moments can be shared with the very young child. More important than the physical presence of parents is the role they play as mediator between the child and the fairy story. A mother or father makes a child feel safe in the presence of giants, hungry wolves, and wicked stepsisters. Yet there is an even more subtle kind of reassurance given to the child by the reading parent. Psychologists tell us that the basis of most fears in early childhood is the child's emerging independence from, and subsequent guilt about, parents. By being present as the child imaginatively kills off wicked stepmothers and replaces them with Prince Charmings, a parent can indicate to children that indulging in fantasies of independence is acceptable. The child can be assured that Mom and Dad will survive these aggressive fantasies, and respond to that simultaneous need to be dependent.

Exercise Two: The Historical Present
Try the conclusion of Sample Essay A, the second last paragraph of Sample Essay B, and Paragraph 7 of Sample Essay C.

Exercise Three: Paragraph Structure and the Controlling Idea
1. Controlling Idea: "There are three groups which have caused the weakening of the Shah's position."

Methods of Organization: classification, some cause and effect, general to specific

Devices for Coherence: parallel structure ("First there are ... Second there are ... Then there are ...") and "Some side ... Others side ... Still others are dedicated ..."), transitional devices (adding ideas: first, second, then; summary words: group, middle-class)

2. Controlling Idea: "Industrial wastes are upsetting nature's balance in every region of this country."

   Methods of Organization: description, specific to general

   Devices for Coherence: parallel structure

3. Controlling Idea: "Beneath the epidermis lies a much thicker portion of the skin — the dermis."

   Methods of Organization: description, general to specific

   Devices for Coherence: pronouns (it, this)

4. Controlling Idea: "The Potlatch Law was difficult to enforce."

   Methods of Organization: narration

   Devices for Coherence: transitional devices (then, however), repeated words (potlatch, law)

Exercise Four: Paragraph Structure and Transitions within Paragraphs

Compare your version to the original in Sample Essay A.

Exercise Five: Paragraph Structure and Transitions within Paragraphs

Paragraph needs better transition between first and second sentence; a possibility might be to begin the second sentence with a subordinate clause: "Since interest groups are so important, one might wonder why they are considerably more predominant in the States than in Canada." Beginning the last sentence of the paragraph with a phrase such as "For the most part" would also make the paragraph move more gracefully.

Exercise Six: Incorporating Quotations in Paragraphs

1. Quotation is incorporated well. Student introduces significance of quotation, quotes, and then explains quotation.

2. Slightly confusing. The connection between the quotation and the comment about Nigeria is not sufficiently explained. Student needs to show that Africa, Nigeria, and Biafra can all be considered nations, depending on how the term nation is defined.

3. Quotation is incorporated well. In particular, the way in which the

student has made reference to the quotation in the sentences which follow it is effective.
4. First quotation is nicely introduced, but not explained well enough in the comments which follow it. The result is that the two quotations seem strung together.

Exercise Seven: Transitions between Paragraphs
Transition between paragraphs one and two: student could show more clearly the priority of the factor being discussed (trivial factor? major factor?)
Paragraph 2 to 3: a "therefore" in the opening sentence of the 3rd paragraph would be helpful
Paragraph 5 to 6: student could introduce new paragraph by noting that she has moved on to another factor
Paragraph 7 to 8: student might make transition to paragraph 8 by showing how it connects to main thesis

Exercise Eight: Introductions
1. Strong introduction which gives background leading to thesis; thesis turns on interesting irony
2. Weak, apologetic introduction which has no thesis and dissolves into confused, illogical, and unrelated details
3. Background, defining terms; thesis is clarified by a contrast between the author's view and that of other writers
4. Controversial quotation with which the author disagrees; effective introduction
5. Too broad, too vague, and undermines the essay
6. Contains a reasonable thesis, but as an introduction is inadequately developed to capture the interest of the reader
7. Empty appreciation of literary work; logical problem with "but" transition; disjointed, inadequate development with only a vague articulation of a possible thesis
8. Too broad; each of the four sentences could be the subject of its own essay
9. Uses question format to define problems and find solutions; workable as long as the essay lives up to the introduction
10. Weak, apologetic, personal, naive-sounding

Exercise Nine: Conclusions
1. Merely restates the thesis

2. Effective conclusion; restates thesis in interesting way and widens scope to consider possible solutions to problem that essay has defined
3. Uses anecdote effectively to illustrate complex thesis
4. Begins with clear statement of thesis, but ends with an analogy so loose that instead of widening the scope, it jumps the track into an unrelated area; try to imagine an analogy that would work better, one that would clearly show the modern knowledge derived from basic research
5. Empty appreciation unrelated to topic of the essay
6. Effective conclusion which widens scope as with a telephoto lens to put problem in a larger context
7. Unnecessarily apologetic; weak
8. Effective summing up of problem along with suggested solutions
9. Effective use of biographical anecdote to cap essay
10. Essay derailed at the last moment by an afterthought which is irrelevant to the major concerns of the essay

Exercise Ten: Introductions and Conclusions
Wilkes' introduction and conclusion work well because they follow the same thesis but express that thesis differently; Progressive movement conclusion is too much a restatement of introduction; introduction and conclusion on school closures work well because conclusion answers questions posed in introduction.

Exercise Eleven: Introductions and Conclusions
Sample Essay A: Introduction is very long, especially when compared to the short conclusion; not particularly clear in the introduction that the student intends to focus on the last eight lines of the poem
Sample Essay B: Introduction could state more clearly the aspects of interest groups the student intends to examine; conclusion could qualify more precisely the current situation of lobby groups in Canada
Sample Essay C: Introduction doesn't suggest clearly the direction that the latter part of this essay will take (environmental factors); as a result, conclusion seems to sum up only the second section of the paper

Exercise Twelve: Revising Syntax through Coordination and Subordination
These sentences can be combined in a variety of ways. One possibility for each of the sentences is listed below.

1. Nuclear power is not only costly, but it also produces potentially deadly wastes which, as of yet, we do not know how to dispose of.
2. When North American Indians suffered from sickness, they recognized these sicknesses as European and therefore would often accept European remedies.
3. If I saw a wild hog foraging in the woods which had a face covered with mud, it would remind me of my brother eating spaghetti.
4. After having spent millions of dollars on research, car manufacturers have developed small horsepower engines that will travel twice as far on a gallon of gas as today's engines.
5. Scientists have a difficult role because, while they must be aware of the advantages of their discoveries, they must be equally aware of the disadvantages.

Exercise Thirteen: Revising Syntax by Employing Parallel Structure

Parallel structure can be fun: play around with these sentences. The examples below give an idea of the possibilities in creative parallel structure.

1. Our goal must be honesty, not fame; our purpose should be to discover the truth rather than to prove ourselves right.
2. We judge our friends by their words and their deeds, but we judge our political representatives by their photo opportunities.
3. Punctuation, then, is analogous to music; commas are the rest signs of a sentence.
4. Shaw's original version was, "We have no more right to consume happiness without producing it, than to consume wealth without making it."
5. One's will reigns at twenty years of age, one's wit at thirty, and one's judgement at forty.

Exercise Fourteen: Revising Diction

1. Short choppy sentences all of the same length and construction; no connections between ideas to indicate relative importance or logical relationships
2. Computerese that may be appropriate to certain technical contexts within the computer world, but comes across as vague, wooden, stilted jargon in the outside world
3. Clear writing; note the precision of this phrasing, its parallel structure and precise logical relationships

4. Self-conscious over-writing; note the overuse of nouns, unnecessary modifiers, and their usual companions, weak verb forms
5. Too casual for rigorous thought or intelligent reader

Exercise Fifteen: Revising Diction
The original paragraph was deliberately exaggerated to show the leaps of logic which could occur when an author uses generalizations instead of concrete words. The following revision establishes the author's line of reasoning more precisely and indeed makes clear the illogicalities of that reasoning.

Both Macbeth and Lady Macbeth share a desire for power more than any other human goal. Although Lady Macbeth seems to persuade Macbeth to commit murder, in fact, both want to accomplish the grisly deed. However, after Duncan has been slain, Macbeth sees ghosts and his wife thinks she cannot wash Duncan's blood from her hands. Finally, the predictions of the witches come true and Macbeth is killed. Hamlet, too, is incited to murder, but he is indecisive about taking such action against Claudius. King Lear was like the Macbeths in that he wanted power, or, more precisely, he wanted power back. Power is also a problem in *Othello,* although one of narrower scope, since Othello primarily wants control over his wife, not a kingdom. This discrepancy in scope has led a few critics to believe that it was Francis Bacon who wrote about the Moor of Venice.

Exercise Sixteen: Revising Grammar
No particular answer

Exercise Seventeen: Revising Grammar
To "sum" an existence, "bound" a life, and find safety in the "strait limits" of an enclosed mind[4] – this *was* the motive of the fictional auto-biographers of Charlotte Brontë's novels. All three autobiographers ["Because" omitted] seem to need to oversimplify both their own natures and the worlds in which they live [second "in" omitted]. They are all different; however, *their methods are* basically the same [exclamation mark omitted]. Repressing what *their* more instinctual impulses tell *them* about the complex truths of experience, [words omitted] they generate personal mythologies by which to rationalize their lives.

Exercise Eighteen: Proofreading

Roughing it in the Bush, Susanna Moodie's witty and moving book about
her experiences in Upper Canada during the 1830s, seems to capture
the essence of Canadian life. However, were it not for the storytelling
skills of another writer, our beloved Susanna might never have come
to Canada. Susanna's husband Dunbar filled his book *Ten Years in South
Africa* with so many tales of danger and mishap that Susanna emphati-
cally refused to accompany him to so terrifying and dangerous a country.
It was unfortunate for the Moodies that Dunbar wrote so convincingly —
they undoubtedly would have fared better there than they did in Canada.

Index